Box Builder's Handbook

A.J. HAMLER

POPULAR WOODWORKING BOOKS
CINCINNATI, OHIO
www.popularwoodworking.com

READ THIS IMPORTANT SAFETY NOTICE

To prevent accidents, keep safety in mind while you work. Use the safety guards installed on power equipment; they are for your protection.

When working on power equipment, keep fingers away from saw blades, wear safety goggles to prevent injuries from flying wood chips and sawdust, wear hearing protection and consider installing a dust vacuum to reduce the amount of airborne sawdust in your woodshop.

Don't wear loose clothing, such as neckties or shirts with loose sleeves, or jewelry, such as rings, necklaces or bracelets, when working on power equipment. Tie back long hair to prevent it from getting caught in your equipment.

People who are sensitive to certain chemicals should check the chemical content of any product before using it.

Due to the variability of local conditions, construction materials, skill levels, etc., neither the author nor Popular Woodworking Books assumes any responsibility for any accidents, injuries, damages or other losses incurred resulting from the material presented in this book.

The authors and editors who compiled this book have tried to make the contents as accurate and correct as possible. Plans, illustrations, photographs and text have been carefully checked. All instructions, plans and projects should be carefully read, studied and understood before beginning construction.

Prices listed for supplies and equipment were current at the time of publication and are subject to change.

METRIC CONVERSION CHART

to convert	to	multiply by
Inches	Centimeters	2.54
Centimeters	Inches	0.4
Feet	Centimeters	30.5
Centimeters	Feet	0.03
Yards	Meters	0.9
Meters	Yards	1.1

BOX BUILDER'S HANDBOOK. Copyright © 2011 by A.J. Hamler. Printed and bound in China. All rights reserved. No part of this book may be reproduced in any form or by any electronic or mechanical means including information storage and retrieval systems without permission in writing from the publisher, except by a reviewer, who may quote brief passages in a review. Published by Popular Woodworking Books, an imprint of F+W Media, Inc., 10150 Carver Rd., Blue Ash, Ohio 45242. (800) 289-0963 First edition.

Distributed in Canada by Fraser Direct
100 Armstrong Avenue
Georgetown, Ontario L7G 5S4
Canada

Distributed in the U.K. and Europe by F&W Media International LTD
Brunel House, Ford Close
Newton Abbot
TQ12 4PU, UK
Tel: (+44) 1626 323200
Fax: (+44) 1626 323319
E-mail: enquiries@fwmedia.com

Distributed in Australia by Capricorn Link
P.O. Box 704
Windsor, NSW 2756
Australia

Visit our Web site at www.popularwoodworking.com.

Other fine Popular Woodworking Books are available from your local bookstore or direct from the publisher.

15   14   13   12   11   5   4   3   2   1

ACQUISITIONS EDITOR: David Thiel
DESIGNER: Brian Roeth
PRODUCTION COORDINATOR: Mark Griffin
PHOTOGRAPHER: A.J. Hamler
ILLUSTRATOR: Jim Stack

ABOUT THE AUTHOR

A.J. Hamler is the former editor of *Woodshop News* and was the founding editor of *Woodcraft Magazine*. As a freelance writer, A.J.'s woodworking articles have appeared in most of the publications in the field and he served as Senior Editor for *The Collins Complete Woodworker* for HarperCollins/Smithsonian. His most recent book is *Easy to Build Birdhouses* from Popular Woodworking Books. When not in his workshop, his other interests include science fiction (writing as A.J. Austin, he's published two novels and numerous short stories), gourmet cooking and Civil War reenactments.

DEDICATION

To Courtney, for whom I've made boxes since the day she was born.

TABLE OF CONTENTS

INTRODUCTION. 6

01 ITTY BITTY BOX. 10

02 WINE BOX 14

03 POST OFFICE BOX 22

04 WATCH BOX. 30

05 TOTE BOX DUO. 36

06 HEART BOX 42

07 POTPOURRI BOX 48

08 LIDDED LATHE BOX 54

09 KIM'S CHRISTMAS BOX 60

10 BEAD BOX 68

11 SPOOL CABINET 74

12 SHAKER OVAL BOX. 84

13 BAND SAW BOX 96

14 PENCIL BOX 104

15 KESTREL BIRD BOX 114

16 BUSINESS CARD HOLDER. 120

17 MAILBOX 126

18 GAME BOX. 136

19 VERTICAL JEWELRY BOX. 150

20 CHILD'S BOX. 164

INTRODUCTION

BOXES, OF ONE KIND OR ANOTHER, HAVE been with humans since forever. Our first were boxes of diapers and infant formula. For our earlier Christmases and birthdays, we were often more fascinated by the box a present came in than the gift itself. A little bit older, and we caught frogs or other small animals and kept them in a cardboard box. As we aged, boxes stayed with us.

Any sports fan reading this is well familiar with box scores and the batter's box, nobody likes to be boxed in, everyone likes to be complimented for thinking outside the box, and who wouldn't want the best seat in the house — a box seat. A few have negative connotations (penalty box, Pandora's box, poor box), but by and large boxes are positive things. It's even been said that life is like a box of chocolates.

It's no mystery that boxes are among the most popular of woodworking projects, and for good reason: They can be designed and used for almost any purpose. Because they use smaller amounts of material, they're economical. Their usually smaller size means that they don't dominate a small workshop, or demand a lot of time. They make perfect gifts.

My goal with the *Box Builder's Handbook* is to present a collection of projects representing a variety of box styles and their associated techniques, and not to teach you how to become a woodworker. But the fact is that boxes are the perfect projects for doing exactly that. Just about all the techniques required for furniture and other larger, more-involved projects can readily be practiced and mastered building boxes.

As you look over the projects in this book, you'll note that it's not intended to serve as an introduction to basic woodworking techniques and tool usage; I'll assume throughout the book that you already have a general understanding of each. But before you get started I wanted to familiarize you with some of the more common methods, materials and tips that you'll use repeatedly.

Joinery

You can use any kind of joinery with boxes, from simple butt joints to intricately cut and fitted dovetails, and plenty in between. This is the perfect time to get up on my soapbox (pun intended) to speak out against one of the more prominent woodworking myths. Chances are good that you've been told repeatedly that butt joints are the weakest of joints and I won't argue that; they are. However, joinery has to be looked at in context — other joinery such as dovetails and mortise-and-tenon are truly strong joints, but you have to consider just how much strength you need.

Sure, you can't really build a very strong table or chair with just butt joints because of the stresses to which they're subjected during use. However, the typical use of boxes involves very little stress to the joinery. Further, wood end-grain — always visible in butt joinery — can often be attractive, especially for some of the more exotic wood species. For that reason, don't be afraid of using butt joints, especially as you practice your skills.

Miter joints are a type of butt joint you'll encounter often in box making, and although not the strongest of joints they're generally plenty strong for boxes as long as you cut them accurately. I recommend ignoring whatever built-in miter scale your saw has and measure miter angles directly on the blade. You can accomplish this with an ordinary pro-tractor, but I rely heavily on a digital angle guide (photo, top left, below). With your blade set exactly, you'll ensure the strongest miter joints possible.

Because these joints work together to create a symmetrical object, and because the miters themselves are symmetrical, they can be very easy to assemble with a common trick: tape. A good, strong tape (I like clear packing tape, which you'll see used repeatedly throughout the projects here) can serve as both assembly aid and clamping mechanism. The process is shown in the sequence of photos 1, 2 & 3 below.

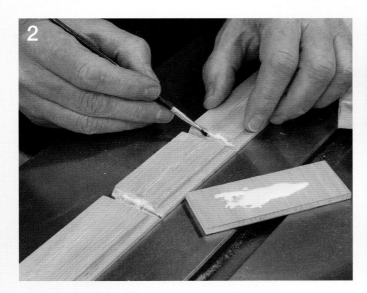

A digital angle meter can give you spot-on adjustments when setting up your table saw for miter cuts, ensuring the tightest-fitting joints possible.

Lay the box sides end-to-end with the outside faces oriented upward. Apply strong packing tape across the back of the miter joints.

Flip the taped components over and dab glue into each of the open miter joints.

Carefully lift and fold the assembly closed. Add a last piece of packing tape to the remaining corner. Check the assembly for square and allow to dry.

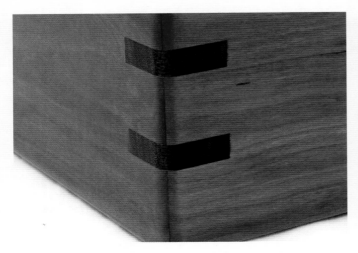

Corner splines add both strength and a decorative touch to mitered boxes.

Internal splines add strength, but are hidden from view inside the joint.

If desired, miter joints can be made stronger and more decorative with corner splines — narrow strips of wood glued into slots made across the joint (photo, top left). Splines add a great deal of mechanical strength to the miter joints, but I'll be honest and admit that I use them mainly for the attractive touch they add. If strength is your only concern, you can create internal splines that run the length of the miter joint instead of across it (photo, top right). These internal splines are invisible from the outside of the box.

Materials

WOOD

You can use just about any wood species imaginable for boxes, and I encourage you to experiment. You'll find that mixing two or three species in a box can be incredibly attractive if the grain and color complement each other. Keep in mind, though, that it's easy to go overboard. Some of the most attractive boxes are very simple; mixing too many species in a single project as small as a box can make it appear busy and overpowering to the eye. There are exceptions, of course, but I recommend you go slowly and carefully when mixing contrasting species.

Again, because boxes are small it's disconcertingly easy to over-design them. When selecting wood, put potential candidates side-by-side to compare grain and color. Keep in mind that the colors will often change drastically once a finish is applied, so when comparing colors it's a good idea to wipe a bit of mineral spirits on the wood to give you an idea of what the finished color will be.

Always do a dry assembly of your boxes before getting out the glue. This way you'll have a better idea of what the final grain orientation will look like and get a preview of how one component will "interact" with another. If it doesn't look right, replace the offending component with another that has a different grain (or with a different species).

LININGS

Not all boxes need a lining, but for those used to house decorative objects — such as jewelry or a watch — a lining can add a touch of both softness and color.

Any soft material works well as a lining, with many box makers favoring felt, velvet, velour and leather. As with wood species, do a dry test with any potential lining by cutting it to fit and putting it exactly where it'll end up in the finished project, then take some time to evaluate it. (This is a good time to bring other family members into the project by getting their opinion.) You might be surprised to see that something that sounded like a good idea on paper just doesn't give the right look. Since the lining isn't permanent at this point, any that doesn't work can easily be replaced with one that does.

Felt and other fabrics can be difficult to mount because they're soft and tend to flap around a lot while you're trying to get it attached, so consider mounting it to another material first (opposite page, top left). Thin cardboard makes a good backing material, and the type used for manila folders is perfect. Glue a slightly over-sized piece of lining to the cardboard, and then trim it for an exact fit. When you have it sized correctly, just glue the cardboard-backed fabric into place. I recently found a kind of felt I've never seen before called stiffened felt. It looks like regular felt but has had sizing added to it, making it into a stiff sheet. It cuts and trims readily, and is very easy to glue into place (opposite page, top right). You can also find felt, velvet and other materials that are self-adhesive with a peel-and-stick backing.

To make felt and other fabrics easier to attach, first glue them to a stiffer material such as cardboard and then trim to fit.

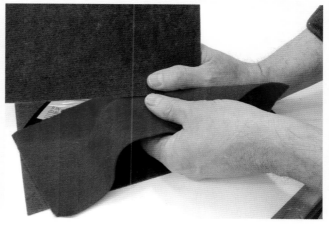

Stiffened felt needs no backing, making it easy to trim to size and glue into your boxes. It's also available in self-stick versions with a peel-off backing.

HARDWARE AND FINISHES

I'm not going to recommend a lot here, as both of these topics are covered more thoroughly with the individual projects. However, just as with other materials, you have a huge range of options, and you should make your choices based on your (or the box recipient's) tastes. I do advise that you try to keep your choices simple whenever possible. As I've already noted, boxes are small and it doesn't take much to overpower them. Proceed carefully with larger-than-needed hinges, ornate pulls or handles, and extremely glossy finishes — once done, these are very difficult to undo if you don't like the look.

SAFETY

It should go without saying that woodworking can be dangerous. There's a safety warning posted at the front of this book, and I'd like to reinforce it here. You may notice that I've removed the guard on my table saw in the photography accompanying the project chapters to make procedures easier to see, but I recommend you use all proper guards and safety equipment intended for your tools. Have adequate

lighting in your work area at all times, and be sure to provide sufficient ventilation when working with glue, stains and volatile finishes. Above all, be sure to protect your eyes and ears.

There are a lot of sharp edges involved in woodworking, but one in particular seems to have popped up only in recent years: staples (see photos below). Because price stickers can fall off, home centers have taken to stapling price tags on the ends of lumber. Be absolutely certain to remove these before working with the lumber, as they can ruin blades if you inadvertently cut through them. If whoever put the staple there wasn't careful, one end of the staple may have missed the wood and be sticking out just waiting to skewer an unsuspecting finger. Even more distressing is the recent practice of applying multiple staples to wood edges. These are applied to "bridge" boards to keep them from sliding as they're stacked and shipped. The problem is that once the boards are separated one end of the staple comes out, resulting in dozens of sharp staple prongs sticking out of board edges. Be on the lookout for these when lumber shopping, and remove them with pliers as soon as you get your lumber home.

To avoid an unexpected cut, be wary of staples driven into board ends and edges. These must be removed before working the lumber with tools.

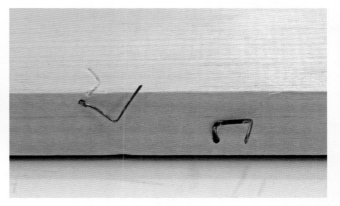

THIS IS PROBABLY THE FASTEST, SIMPLEST project in the book, but it's far from simple looking. I've made quite a few of these little beauties over the years, because I'm one of those guys who doesn't like store packaging. Frequently, when buying a gift of jewelry for my wife, I've just tossed out the original packaging and created a small box I liked better. In fact, I think this particular little box is the first I've ever made that wasn't associated with a specific gift. (Which means, of course, that I'll have to stash this away until the appropriate gift comes along.)

01 ITTY BITTY BOX

Since I made this without intending it to contain a particular item, I pretty much sized it randomly based on the stock I had on hand, but if you plan to create one for a gift box, do what I do. Get the gift first, then remove the mounting material from inside the packaging. Most jewelry, from earrings to necklaces, usually come with a flocked or velvety sort of cardboard insert that is slotted or perforated to hold the jewelry, then folded to fit the box it came in. If you've bought jewelry with this kind of insert, remove it from the original package and measure it carefully, then create your little box so you can slip this insert inside. The jewelry will look stunning inside your handcrafted box.

One thing to keep in mind here is that this project is very small, which means you'll be cutting components that are even smaller. Be extremely careful doing this. To make cutting safer, I've elected to make larger master workpieces for the more dangerous cuts, and then cut the individual parts from this larger one.

Construction

To start, take a piece of stock long enough to create all four box sides, plus a bit more, then rip it to the length of the box sides at 2⅛". Then, set the blade on your table saw to 45° to cut a miter down each side of the piece, as in Fig. 1.

After returning the blade to 90°, slice off the four sides using a miter gauge (Fig. 2). If you have any trepidation about working and mitering small pieces like this, or working close to the blade, then simply don't do it. You can also make miters for a box this small on a disc sander by setting the sander's table to 45°.

Assembling this little mitered box is easy. For larger boxes, I'd probably use packing tape to hold the corners as I folded the box closed, but I find it more straightforward with boxes of this size to simply glue the corners and hold the box

REFERENCE	QUANTITY	PART	STOCK	THICKNESS	(mm)	WIDTH	(mm)	LENGTH	(mm)	COMMENTS
A	1	lid	walnut burl	$1/4$	(6)	$2^1/8$	(54)	$2^1/8$	(54)	
B	1	lid keeper	walnut burl	$1/4$	(6)	$1^5/8$	(41)	$1^5/8$	(41)	
C	4	sides	walnut burl	$1/4$	(6)	$1^1/4$	(32)	$2^1/8$	(54)	
D	1	bottom	walnut burl	$1/4$	(6)	$1^5/8$	(41)	$1^5/8$	(41)	

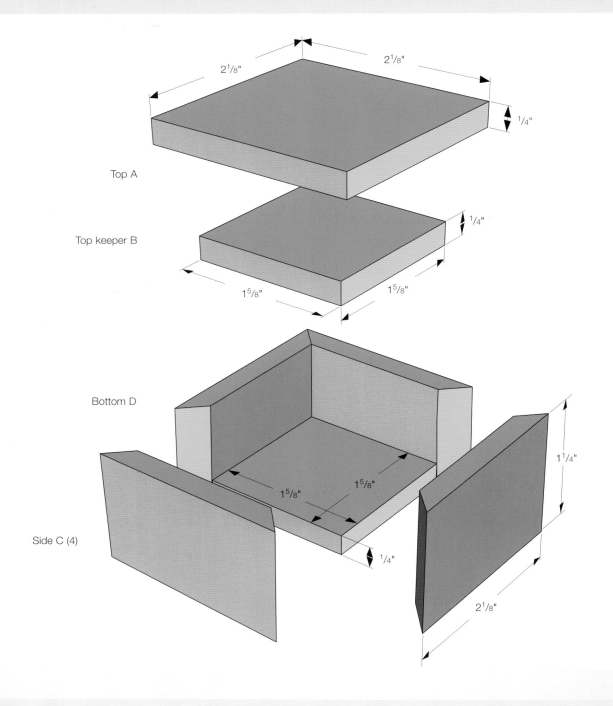

Top A

Top keeper B

Bottom D

Side C (4)

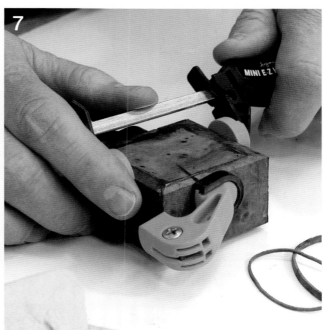

in shape for a minute or two with my fingers before slipping on a few stiff rubber bands to clamp it, as in Fig. 3. As with any box, be sure to check for square when doing your glue-up.

While the glue sets, cut the box bottom and lid keeper to size. Check the fit and mark the best orientation as in Fig. 4, then set the bottom aside for now. Glue the lid keeper on the underside of the inverted lid, and before the glue sets slip the box over the lid to position the keeper for a perfect fit (Fig. 5).

Allow the glue to set up for a few minutes, then remove the box and clamp the lid keeper in place till dry (Fig. 6).

Apply a bit of glue to the edges of the box bottom and slip it into place on your marks. If needed, clamp the box to keep the bottom in place, but apply only the smallest amount of pressure necessary. As you can see in Fig. 7, I'm using the tiniest clamps I own for the task.

Finish the box any way you like — I've used a wiping varnish — and then slip the insert from your original jewelry packing inside for a stunning presentation. If you've made the box with no particular gift or insert in mind, adding a lining to the bottom of the box would be a nice touch.

MOST TRUE WINE AFICIONADOS TEND TO turn their noses up at wine that comes in a box; for them, only the finest bottled wine will do. However, I'm willing to bet that anyone who loves wine will enjoy any vintage that arrives in this box.

Containers to carry wine bottles aren't unique — any Internet search will turn up numerous bags, pouches, boxes and other containers — but the thing I noticed about almost all of these was that they're intended for just a single purpose: carrying a bottle of wine. This means that should you gift a friend a boxed bottle, after enjoying the wine itself the box will end up on a shelf until needed to carry a bottle once more. I got to thinking, wouldn't it be nicer if a wine box were designed to have another purpose after fulfilling its original job? Seems to me that would certainly beat tossing it up on a shelf to collect dust.

That's exactly what I've done with this project. For its original purpose of carrying a gift of wine to a friend, the bottle fits inside and is held in place by a keeper. The keeper extends about ⅜" above the top of the open box, allowing the lid to nestle over the top.

Once the box is empty, however, flip the keeper over and it becomes an inner tray. The lid fits over the tray the same way, but now the box can be used for just about any purpose, with a larger main compartment underneath and a shallow lift-out tray resting above.

As with some of the other boxes in this book created to contain specific items, always start by getting an exact measurement. The bottle I used measured 12" high and 3" in diameter, which is about average for wine bottles. Using that measurement, I added a bit to each dimension for some extra room (just in case someone came along and drank the wine from my intended bottle before I finished the project, there'd be enough room in the box for a bottle of similar size). You'll notice from the cut list that other than the lid insert, there are no components listed for the lid. That's because we'll build the box as a single unit, then cut the lid free from the box. This method of making the lid is not only easier, but it guarantees a perfect fit, as well as continuous grain between the box and lid sides.

02 WINE BOX

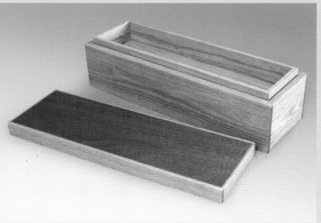

The Wine Box lid is held on by the internal tray. Turn the tray upside down over the wine bottle to hold it securely. Later, flip the tray right side up for other uses.

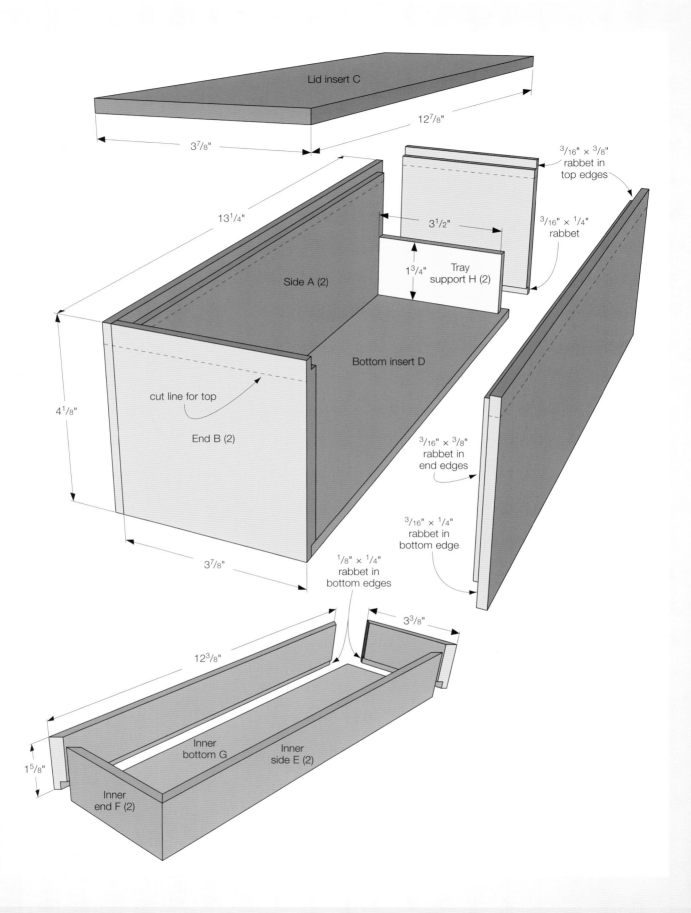

Lid insert C

12⁷/₈"

3⁷/₈"

³/₁₆" × ³/₈"
rabbet in
top edges

13¹/₄"

3¹/₂"

³/₁₆" × ¹/₄"
rabbet

Side A (2)

1³/₄"   Tray
support H (2)

4¹/₈"

Bottom insert D

cut line for top

End B (2)

³/₁₆" × ³/₈"
rabbet in
end edges

3⁷/₈"

³/₁₆" × ¹/₄"
rabbet in
bottom edge

¹/₈" × ¹/₄"
rabbet in
bottom edges

3³/₈"

12³/₈"

Inner
bottom G

Inner
side E (2)

1⁵/₈"

Inner
end F (2)

WINE BOX • INCHES (MILLIMETERS)

REFERENCE	QUANTITY	PART	STOCK	THICKNESS	(mm)	WIDTH	(mm)	LENGTH	(mm)	COMMENTS
A	2	sides	oak	$3/8$	(10)	$4^1/8$	(105)	$13^1/4$	(336)	
B	2	ends	oak	$3/8$	(10)	$4^1/8$	(105)	$3^7/8$	(98)	
C	1	lid insert	mahongany	$1/4$	(6)	$3^7/8$	(98)	$12^7/8$	(327)	
D	1	bottom insert	oak ply	$1/4$	(6)	$3^7/8$	(98)	$12^7/8$	(327)	
E	2	inner tray sides	oak	$1/4$	(6)	$1^5/8$	(41)	$12^3/8$	(315)	
F	2	inner tray ends	oak	$1/4$	(6)	$1^5/8$	(41)	$3^3/8$	(86)	
G	1	inner tray bottom	oak ply	$1/4$	(6)	$3^1/8$	(79)	$12^1/8$	(308)	
H	2	tray supports	oak	$1/4$	(6)	$1^3/4$	(45)	$3^1/2$	(89)	

Construction

After cutting the parts, it's a good idea to recheck for size before you start working (Fig. 1). We'll divide this box into two projects — the main box, and the tray insert.

Start construction of the main box by cutting $3/16$" × $3/8$" rabbets on each end of both sides, as I'm doing with a dado set in my table saw in Fig. 2. If you prefer, you can cut the rabbets with a straight bit in a table-mounted router. Now, adjust the dado set or router table to cut $3/16$" × $1/4$" rabbets on the top and bottom edges of both sides, as well as the top and bottom edges of the end pieces (Fig. 3).

Spread glue into the end rabbets on the box sides, (Fig. 4) and clamp the main box together (Fig. 5). Although I'm not yet gluing it in place, I'm dropping in the mahogany lid insert, which I know is square, to keep things aligned while the glue dries.

Once dry, pop out the insert, add glue to the top rabbets and drop the insert into place. Arrange a few wooden blocks around the edge of the insert to act as cauls to spread the pressure evenly when you clamp the insert, as in Fig. 6, and allow to dry. Unclamp the box and flip it upside down, then glue in the bottom insert the same way you did for the lid. When you've got the bottom insert securely clamped, immediately turn the assembly right side up. I'll explain why in a moment.

First, a few notes on this method of box/lid construction are in order since it will pop up again in later projects. Since you're effectively making an elongated sealed cube, you might be wondering how you contain or wipe up any glue squeeze-out on the inside. The answer is, you can't. That's why when doing this kind of box I always glue in the lid component first, which allows me to reach through the bottom while the assembly is clamped and get rid of any extra glue that squeezes out. Using glue sparingly helps, too. The inside of a box lid rarely receives additional adornment such as a lining, so cleaning any squeeze-out there is a priority. The bottom, though, is often a different story. You still want to avoid squeeze-out by using glue sparingly, but by doing the bottom insert last you can minimize the effects of any squeeze-out later when you add a liner — any glue you can't remove once the lid is cut off will be hidden beneath your lining.

Remember earlier when I told you to immediately turn the box right side up while the glue for the bottom insert dried? This keeps any extra glue from dripping down the inside toward the lid.

Now, let's remove that lid. You can do this on the band saw — and we'll do it that way in a later project — but let's use the table saw here. The box sides are ³⁄₈" thick, so set the blade height just a hair shy of that. Now set the fence distance to create a lid of the desired height; in this case, ³⁄₄". Be sure to allow for the blade kerf when setting your fence. (Since the completed height of this box is 4", you'll note that I've allowed an extra ¹⁄₈" on the cut list for the box sides and ends to account for the blade kerf.)

Start cutting on one of the ends, using a piece of scrap as a push block as in Fig. 7. Because the box is taller in this orientation than it is long, using a push block when cutting the ends allows for more control of the cut. Now just work your way around the box until all four sides are cut (Fig. 8).

Since we set the blade height just shy of the thickness of the sides, the lid is still attached. Again, this was for safety reasons; you don't want the lid flying free on that last cut. To remove the lid, just cut through the remaining thin portion with a sharp utility knife as I'm doing in Fig. 9, while holding the lid. When the lid is free, use the knife and a sanding block to clean up any remaining material (Fig. 10).

The last thing the main box needs before moving on to the tray is to add the two tray supports on the ends by gluing and clamping them into position (Fig. 11).

The tray goes together quickly using miter joints. After cutting the miters on the ends of each of the tray sides, lay them, miter down, on a flat surface (the top of my table saw works well for this) and use packing tape to temporarily hold the miters together (Fig. 12). Keep the edge of the miters tight while applying the tape.

When all four pieces are taped (remember the proper order), except for the last joint, flip the taped piece over and apply glue to the miter joints (Fig. 13).

With glue on all the miters, fold the pieces together to form the rectangle of the tray, and tape the last miter joint tight (Fig. 14).

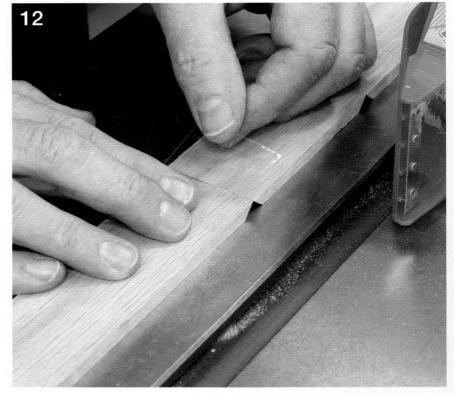

Although I've used packing tape to assembly the tray, I've opted for a bit more clamping strength with a band clamp, as in Fig. 15. Just as with the mahogany lid insert, you can drop the bottom into place to keep the assembly square. Once the tray dries, glue the bottom into place permanently as you did with the bottom of the main box earlier.

Since this box will be toted around and may receive some rough handling, after finish-sanding all the pieces, I opted for a couple coats of polyurethane. When the finish was dry, I added a felt liner in the bottom of the main box that not only cushions the wine bottle that will go inside, but gives the box a nice final appearance. Adding a liner to the bottom of the tray insert is up to you.

À votre santé!

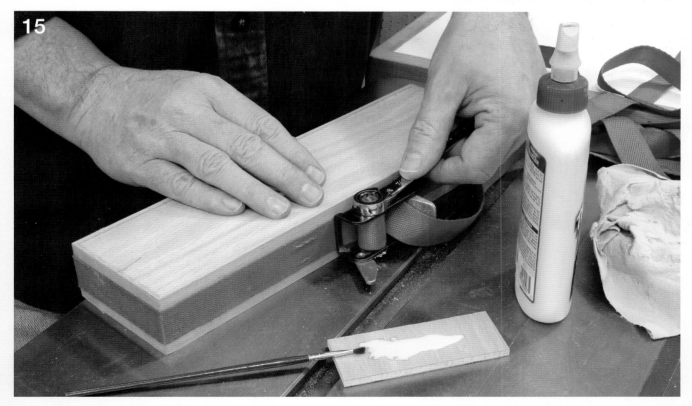

ONCE CREATED, ALMOST ANY PROJECT CAN have the word "box" appended to it as a means of describing its purpose. For some, the word is already an official part of the name, such as mailbox, breadbox or jewelry box. But there's only one project in this book that has the word attached to it before you even start to make it, and that describes this bank made from an old Post Office (or P.O.) box door.

Private mailboxes in most post offices these days constitute a featureless ugly wall of aluminum, with each compartment requiring a key. These modern boxes show little attempt at an attractive design, and have all the charm of aluminum siding.

But once upon a time, P.O. boxes were works of art that incorporated embossed lettering, such as a stylish "U.S." A bas-relief graphic of an eagle spreading its wings was also common, as were angled rays or starbursts. These boxes were usually brass or bronze — although occasionally zinc or, more rarely, steel — with the raised portions polished bright and the surrounding background a matte enamel finish that made the sculpted portion stand out handsomely. Even the later designs, although simpler, were still manufactured in bronze and included graphic flourishes.

Combination locks where mostly the rule from the late 1800s to the mid 20th century, with keyed

doors appearing in the '50s and '60s. Many of the earlier keyed bronze P.O. box doors were simply re-conditioned combination single-dial models with the locking mechanism switched out — the combination letters cast in the doors were still there, but an incongruous keyhole now appeared in the center instead of the twist dial. The last bronze doors were made up to around 1970, with those ugly aluminum ones taking over after that.

P.O. boxes were usually available in three sizes, numbered 1 through 3, with the No. 1 door — measuring approximately 3½" × 5" — being the most common. However, even though No. 1 doors were nominally the same size on the front, there were slight size variations on the back, as well as different mounting methods. This is important to remember. The dimensions I've given in the cut list on page 25 exactly fit the door you see in the photographs, but may be slightly too large or too small for another door, particularly in width. For this reason, it's essential that you acquire your door before you start cutting the stock. I discuss some particulars of P.O. box doors in the sidebar, "Working Door-to-Door" on Page 29.

03 POST OFFICE BOX

Construction

Since the bottom and both sides of this box are the same depth and use the same-sized rabbet, it's easiest to cut a single 15½"-long workpiece to the box depth of 4½" and then cut a continuous ¼" × ⅜" rabbet on one edge in a single pass as in Fig. 1. I've used a dado cutter in my table saw to make these rabbets, but you can use a router table or do them by hand with a rabbeting plane.

Once you've milled the rabbet, you'll find that your 15½" workpiece will yield the bottom and both sides of one box, once crosscut to the correct lengths. Of course, if you plan to make more than one box, you can make this workpiece as long as you like — a 31" workpiece will provide components for two boxes, a 46½" piece will make three boxes, etc.

Mill a ⅜" × ⅝" rabbet on the bottoms of each side piece, taking care to correctly orient the back rabbets you cut earlier. At this point, it's a good idea to do a dry-fit of the three components to

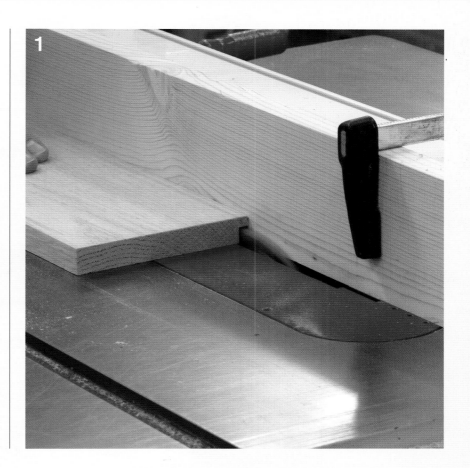

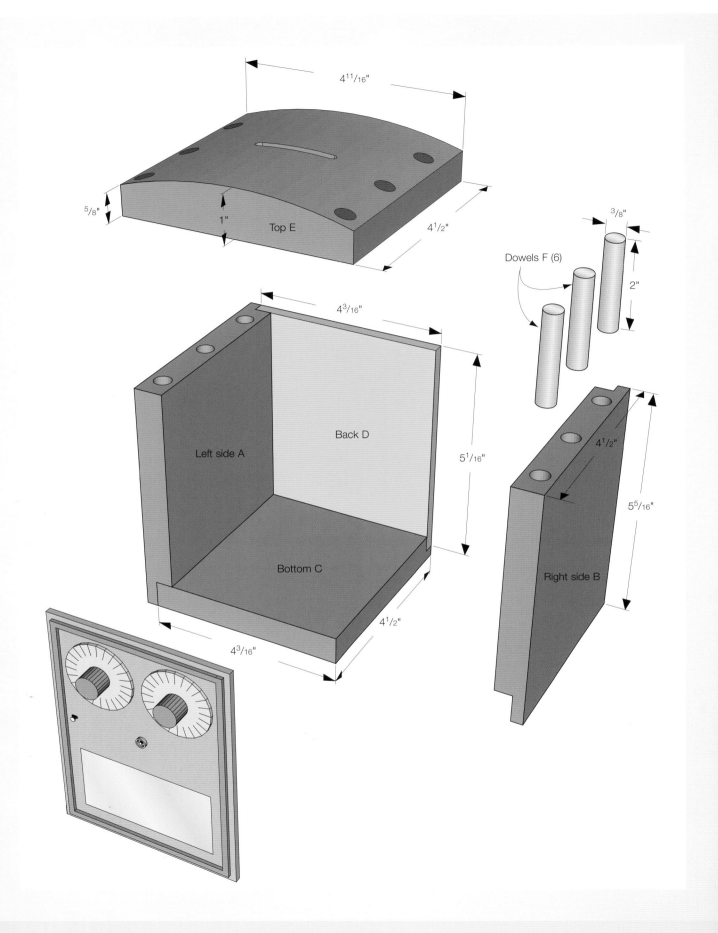

4¹¹/₁₆"

5/8"

1"

Top E

4¹/₂"

3/8"

Dowels F (6)

2"

4³/₁₆"

Left side A

Back D

5¹/₁₆"

4¹/₂"

Right side B

5⁵/₁₆"

Bottom C

4¹/₂"

4³/₁₆"

REFERENCE	QUANTITY	PART	STOCK	THICKNESS	(mm)	WIDTH	(mm)	LENGTH	(mm)	COMMENTS
A	1	left side	oak	$5/8$	(8)	$4^{1}/_2$	(115)	$5^{5}/_{16}$	(135)	Measure door to confirm
B	1	right side	oak	$5/8$	(8)	$4^{1}/_2$	(115)	$5^{5}/_{16}$	(135)	Measure door to confirm
C	1	bottom	oak	$5/8$	(8)	$4^{1}/_2$	(115)	$4^{3}/_{16}$	(110)	Measure door to confirm
D	1	back	oak	$1/4$	(6)	$4^{3}/_{16}$	(110)	$5^{5}/_{16}$	(135)	Measure door to confirm
E	1	top	oak	1	(25)	$4^{1}/_2$	(115)	$4^{11}/_{16}$	(119)	Measure door to confirm
F	6	dowels	oak	$3/8$	(10)	2	(51)			
G	1	box door	bronze/brass	–	–	$3^{1}/_2$	(89)	5	(127)	Dimensions vary
H	1	coin slot cover	brass	–	–	$1^{5}/_8$	(41)	$1^{5}/_8$	(41)	Dimensions vary

check the fit of your door. In Fig. 2, I've clamped the bottom and sides together and slipped the door into position. If the door fits too loosely, cut a bit off one side edge of the bottom piece, which will bring the two sides closer together for a better fit. Likewise, if the door is just a hair too snug, you can probably enlarge the opening a bit by coarse-sanding the edges of the opening where the door makes contact with the wood. However, if the door simply won't fit into the opening it's best to make a new bottom piece that's a bit larger. (Save this mis-sized piece, however — with the variation in sizes among old doors it may fit another door perfectly.)

While you still have the box clamped up, flip it over and mark the screw holes for attaching the door frame as I'm doing in Fig. 3. With the clamped-up box still inverted, cut and fit the ¼"-thick back panel and slide it into place to check the fit. When you're satisfied that the back and door fit perfectly, unclamp the box and drill pilot holes for the screws on the marks you made. With the pilot holes drilled, apply glue to the rabbets and assemble the bottom, sides and back, and then clamp up the assembly.

Cut the 1"-thick top to size. Hold your coin slot cover on the top and trace its opening onto the wood, centered on the top. If you have a hollow-chisel mortiser you can use it to quickly cut the slot into the top. Alternatively, you can do as I've done here and drill a series of ³⁄₁₆" holes along your mark and then clean up the slot with a sharp bench chisel (Fig. 4). While the width of this slot isn't critical — it's fine to make it wider than the actual opening in the brass slot cover to accommodate the size of the mortiser chisel or drill bit you use to cut it — but don't make it any longer. The brass slot cover is held on with a pair of escutcheon pins set very close to the ends of the opening, so you don't have a lot of room to work with for the pins. Glue the top to the box and clamp in place, as in Fig. 5.

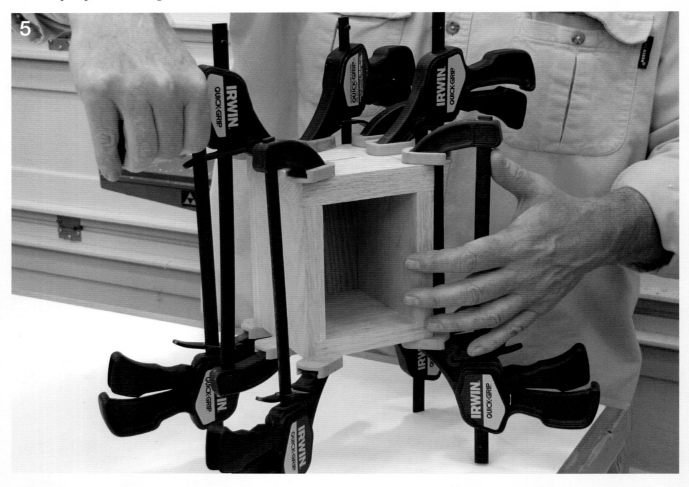

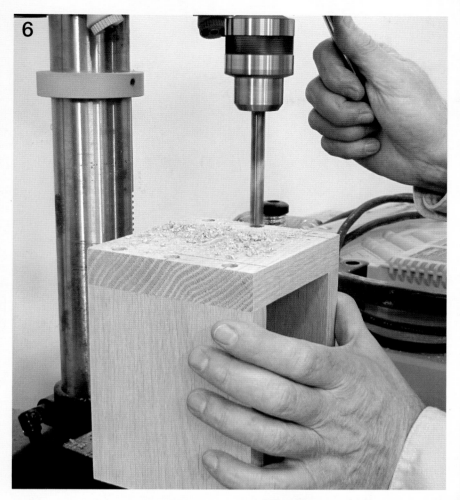

When the box has dried, remove the clamps and mark each side of the top for three evenly spaced ³/₈" dowels. Take care to place these marks so they fall exactly within the width of the sides, then drill ³/₈" holes about 1³/₄" deep into the top of the box and down into the sides. (Fig. 6) Apply a bit of glue into the holes and drive the dowels into place as in Fig. 7.

When the dowels have dried, draw a curved line on the top-front of the box, and use your band saw to cut the arch, as in Fig. 8. Follow with a thorough sanding, either with a disc sander as I'm doing in Fig. 9, or with a hand sander.

At this point the box is ready to be stained and finished however you please, although I recommend a polyurethane topcoat for durability — this box will be handled a lot. When the finish is dry, attach the coin slot cover with escutcheon pins.

Before you attach the door make sure you have the combination recorded and kept somewhere safe; in fact, it's a good idea while working to write the combination on the door's glass with a grease pencil. Once the door is mounted you're not getting it off again without the combination. Got that combination saved? Good. Now, and only now screw the door frame into place. A driver with a standard bit probably won't do you much good here, but an extra-long bit in your driver or a very short screwdriver will make the task easier. Note in Fig. 10 that I've used a bit of folded paper towel to prevent the opened door from rubbing on the finish while I screw the door on.

Working Door-to-Door

P.O. box doors came in a huge variety till about 1900 with designs, sizes and mounting methods all over the board, but by the 20th century standardization set in with two frontrunners in door styles. The most common door in the first part of the century was the one I've used for this box project: the two-dial combination door made by the Corbin Cabinet Lock Co. of New Britain, Conn. This door featured a four-sided rear frame that mounted into a box with a single screw through each of the four sides of the frame. This door generally fit into an opening measuring $3^7/_{16}$" x $4^5/_8$", but there were some very slight size variations depending on year of manufacture. If using this type of door you'll need to measure and cut your bank box carefully to ensure a snug but smooth fit. This is a truly handsome door, but not always easy to find. Expect to pay at least $20-$25 for one in good shape. By the 1950s a newer style appeared that was easier to mass-produce with fewer variations. Known as the "Grecian" style for the scrollwork around the edges, this single-dial door was simpler than the earlier Corbins, but still attractive. Although produced by more than one manufacturer, government standards made Grecian doors more consistent in size. These doors fit an opening of about $3^3/_{16}$" x $4^5/_8$", and instead of the four-sided rear frame they used a pair of drilled tabs on each side as attachment points. These tabs make your work easier — if the door fits just a little too tight or a little too loose, the tabs can be bent slightly for a better fit. Also, because the mounting tabs are only on the sides, just the horizontal measurement of the box opening is critical — no screws are located top or bottom, allowing for a bit of vertical wiggle room. More common than the old Corbins, Grecian doors usually sell for around $10-$25. I've included a few sources below for purchasing doors, but your best bet is to check local antique stores and flea markets, as well as eBay, for door bargains.

R.P & COMPANY HISTORICAL COIN BANKS
P.O. Box 269
Errol, NH 03579
(603) 482-3252
www.rpcompany.com
(Two-dial and Grecian combination doors, number decals, slots)

PEN MAKING SUPPLIES
P.O. Box 607
Peapack, NJ 07977
(908) 204-0095
www.penmakingsupplies.com
(Grecian combination doors, coin slots)

ROCKLER
(800) 279-4441
www.rockler.com
(Grecian keyed doors, coin slots)

I MENTIONED EARLIER THAT I DON'T CARE much for the packaging most jewelry comes in, so I frequently make my own. This Watch Box project is a case in point. The watch you see in the photos is the oldest gift my wife has from me: I bought it for her birthday the first year we were married back in the '70s. (Yes, yes; that was way in the last century, back in the days of disco and leisure suits.) It's obviously a very good watch — it's lasted many decades — and it's probably her favorite, but at the time I had no woodworking tools to speak of. Creating a custom box for it wasn't possible then, but when I was putting together a project list for this book it occurred to me that a box for her watch was something I'd never gotten around to doing. Sure, I like to make these boxes when I give the gifts, but nothing says I can't make one after the fact. Come to that, I'm surprised I'd not made this one earlier.

04 WATCH BOX

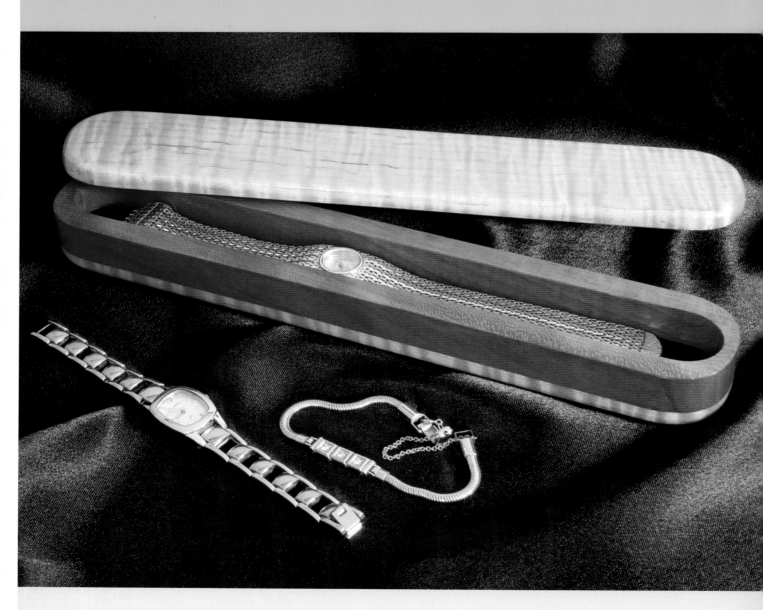

Construction

I had a small piece of tiger maple I'd been saving, so I decided to resaw it to create the top and bottom of the box as in Fig. 1, and although the box body would separate the two pieces, the heavy figuring would still be continuous top to bottom. If you decide to do the same, after creating the two matched pieces make a few marks on the ends to remind you of the correct orientation, then clean up the resawn faces on the jointer as in Fig. 2. Lacking a jointer, you can handle the task easily with a belt sander or random orbit sander, or by hand with a sanding block.

To size the opening you'll need for the watch (or bracelet), lay it atop the workpiece of the box body and simply trace around it as in Fig. 3. Allow a bit of extra space on each side to accommodate the winding stem. (Yes, this watch is old enough that it doesn't use a battery.) Also allow a bit of extra room on the ends to make reaching into the box easier. For this watch, I decided that an opening 1" wide by 9¼" long was optimal, but adjust your opening to fit your specific watch. Also, be sure to take the height of the watch into consideration when sizing the workpiece of the box body — the depth will need to accommodate the watch as well as the ⅛" lid keeper.

WATCH BOX • INCHES (MILLIMETERS)

REFERENCE	QUANTITY	PART	STOCK	THICKNESS	(mm)	WIDTH	(mm)	LENGTH	(mm)	COMMENTS
A	1	lid	figured maple	1/4	(6)	1 3/4	(45)	10	(254)	
B	1	lid keeper	figured maple	1/8	(3)	1	(25)	9 1/4	(235)	
C	1	box body	mahogany	5/4	(16)	1 3/4	(45)	10	(254)	
D	1	bottom	figured maple	1/4	(6)	1 3/4	(45)	10	(254)	

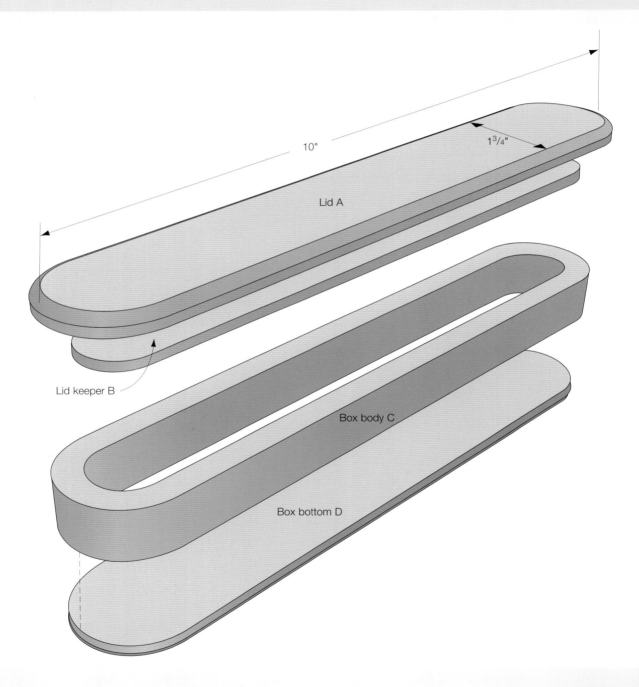

10"

1 3/4"

Lid A

Lid keeper B

Box body C

Box bottom D

You can start by drilling both ends of the opening with an appropriately sized Forstner bit, then connect the two holes. A scroll saw would work best for this, but I don't have one; however, since a cut through end-grain is all but invisible when glued back together, I opted to do this on the band saw as in Fig. 4, by just cutting right through the ends. After cutting the opening, cut through the opposite end to separate the two halves — this way the amount of kerf removed will be equal on both ends — then glue and clamp the box body back together.

When the glue has dried, smooth out the inside of the opening with a spindle sander, as in Fig. 5, then glue the bottom to the box body (Fig. 6). Note that I'm using the loose lid as a clamping caul to evenly distribute the clamping force. In Fig. 7 I'm trimming the box assembly on the table saw after the glue has dried.

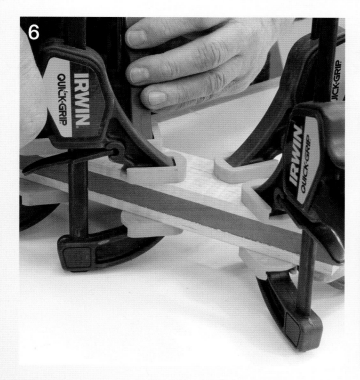

Temporarily attach the box lid with packing tape and round each end. A band saw works perfectly for this (Fig. 8), but you can also use a scroll saw or jigsaw. Sand the curve smooth with a disc sander (Fig. 9), or by hand (Fig. 10).

Give the bottom edge of the box and the edge of the lid a soft curve using a roundo-

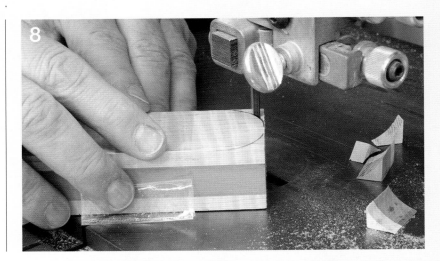

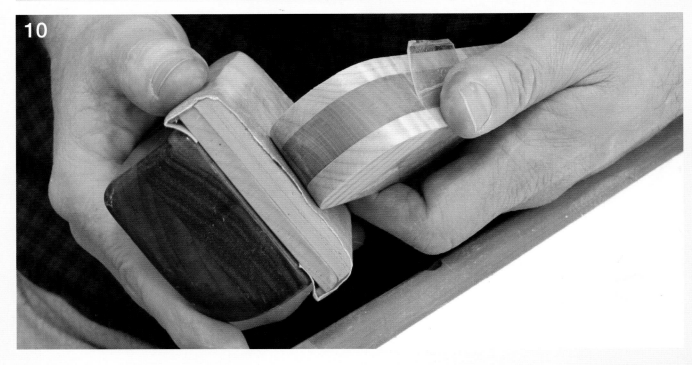

ver bit in the router table as in Fig. 11. Do this very careful, taking your time. If you have any doubts at all about working this closely with a router, then create this roundover by hand using a combination of a file and hand sanding. Or, if you prefer, you can skip the roundover and leave the box edges sharply angled.

The last step is to set the lid keeper by gluing it to the underside of the lid, and positioning it exactly by slipping the box body over it and allowing the glue to set up for a few minutes, as in Fig. 12. Then remove the box body and clamp the lid keeper in place securely till dry.

Give the completed watch box a glossy or satin finish — a wiping varnish works well for this — then add a felt or velvet liner to the inside of the box. Because I wanted a high contrast to the watch's silver color I chose a black felt, but you can pick whatever color you feel best complements the watch lucky enough to occupy the box.

THESE TOTE BOXES OR CARRYALLS HAVE BEEN around for hundreds of years, with almost as many variations. Carpenters of old made sturdy examples out of local hardwoods designed to take a beating — they were rarely careful when tossing their tools in or dropping the box down before getting to work. In more modern times the basic design has become a staple of country-style decorating with lighter and softer wood species taking the place of bulletproof hardwoods, and the wood adorned with paint, stencil-ing and decoupage. No box book is complete without a tote box, but which one to choose? I couldn't pick between them, so I decided to include both.

The components for these two totes are nearly the same, although I've made a few adjustments to account for the differing thicknesses of the stock — I've used ½" oak for the "Classic" style box, and off-the-shelf ¾" pine for the "Country" version. The beginning steps of both versions are the same, so we'll cover them here simultaneously.

05 TOTE BOX DUO

Construction

Begin by cutting out the shaped ends. This is most easily accomplished by cutting both ends in pairs at the same time, resulting in perfectly matched pieces. Whichever tote you're making, attach two slightly oversized pieces of stock together with brads, then transfer the appropriate end pattern onto your stacked pieces. In Fig. 1, I've opted to cut these out on the band saw, but a scroll saw or handheld jigsaw can also handle the task quickly. Cut out the entire pattern except the flat bottom, leaving the two pieces attached for now.

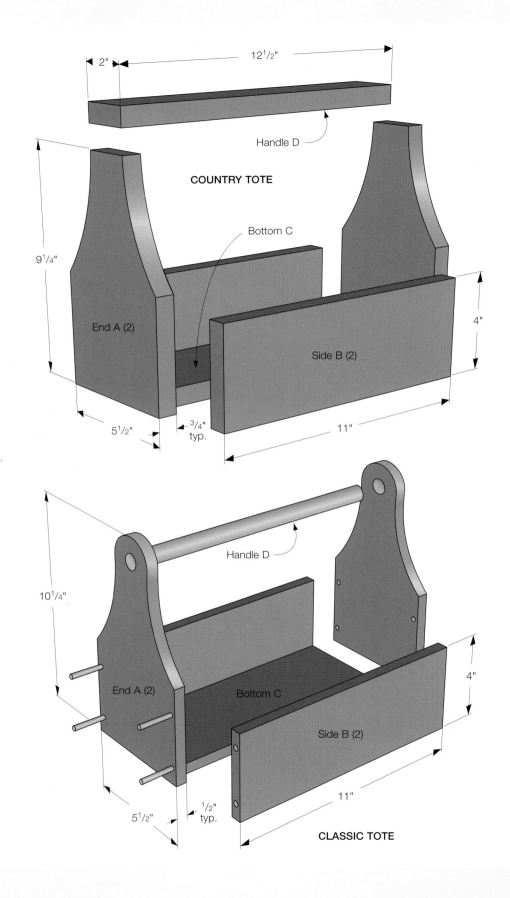

2"

12$\frac{1}{2}$"

Handle D

COUNTRY TOTE

Bottom C

9$\frac{1}{4}$"

End A (2)

Side B (2)

4"

5$\frac{1}{2}$"

$\frac{3}{4}$"
typ.

11"

Handle D

10$\frac{1}{4}$"

End A (2)

Bottom C

Side B (2)

4"

5$\frac{1}{2}$"

$\frac{1}{2}$"
typ.

11"

CLASSIC TOTE

TOTE BOX • INCHES (MILLIMETERS)

REFERENCE	QUANTITY	PART	STOCK	THICKNESS	(mm)	WIDTH	(mm)	LENGTH	(mm)	COMMENTS
CLASSIC TOTE										
A	2	ends	oak	1/2	(13)	5 1/2	(140)	10 1/4	(260)	
B	2	sides	oak	1/2	(13)	4	(102)	11	(279)	
C	1	bottom	oak	1/2	(13)	4 1/2	(115)	11	(279)	
D	1	handle	oak dowel	3/4	(19)	12	(305)			
COUNTRY TOTE										
A	2	ends	pine	3/4	(19)	5 1/2	(140)	9 1/4	(209)	
B	2	sides	pine	3/4	(19)	4	(102)	11	(279)	
C	1	bottom	pine	3/4	(19)	4	(102)	11	(279)	
D	1	handle	pine	3/4	(19)	2	(51)	12 1/2	(318)	

Clean up the shape by sanding. All the outside curves can be done on a disc sander as in Fig. 2, while an oscillating spindle sander nicely handles the concave edges (Fig. 3).

With all edges sanded smooth, make the last cut on the bottom edge squarely on the table saw, as in Fig. 4. At this point, the two versions of this project diverge a bit. Let's look at the Classic Tote first, which is made of harder wood and with a bit more strength.

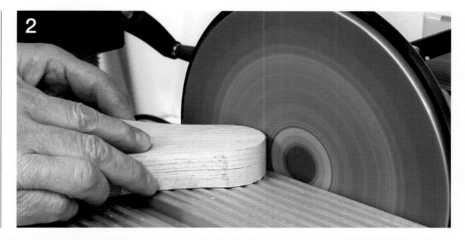

Glue the bottom into place between the two sides as in Fig. 5. This edge-to-face glue joint is very strong, and needs no mechanical reinforcement in a box this size. (I'll have some thoughts on altering this design for a larger box at the end of the chapter.) You can see in this photo that I've already drilled the ¾" holes in the tops of the end pieces to accept the dowel handle. If you haven't drilled these yet, now's a good time. Use a drill press if you have one to ensure perfect 90° holes; if you use a handheld drill, take care that the holes are perfectly vertical.

When the box body has dried, glue both ends in place and clamp up till dry. I noted that we were going to make this a strong little box — I plan to carry some small but heavy tools in it — so reinforce the ends with dowels as in Fig. 6. I'm using Miller Dowels, a unique stepped dowel, but regular ¼" dowels will also work. Drill a pair of evenly spaced holes on each side of both ends. Squirt in a bit of glue and hammer the dowels home, then trim any protruding dowel with a fine-cut saw and sand smooth. The last step for this Classic Tote is to glue the dowel handle into place. I've relied just on glue to hold the dowel into place, but for extra strength you might consider drilling and driving an additional dowel down through the top of the end pieces and into the dowel to secure it.

Those old-time carpenters probably left the wood raw more often than not, but I chose to top my Classic Tote off with a few coats of polyurethane.

Now let's take a look at how the Country Tote goes together.

As I noted at the outset, to be able to use the same end pattern for both boxes I've altered a few of the stock dimensions. The two main differences are that the tops of the end pieces are flat to accept a flat handle instead of a dowel, and the bottom is a bit narrower. Cut the bottom to 4" wide as in Fig. 7. This will

slim the width a bit to keep the thicker ¾" sides within the 5½" end pieces when assembled.

Attach the side pieces to the box bottom with glue and brads as in Fig. 8, then attach the ends the same way. Then attach the handle to the top, again with glue and brads (Fig. 9).

Give the completed tote a light sanding — for country-style decorating, a really fine sanding usually isn't necessary or even always desirable — and follow up with the paint or other decorations of your choice. If you enjoy stenciling, this is the perfect project for it.

I always encourage readers to use my plans and dimensions as a guide or starting point, and to alter any of the projects as dictated by the imagination. As such, this is one of the most customizable projects in this book. Classic totes of this type came in a huge range of sizes — I've seen some in antique stores measuring four feet long and more — so alter any dimension you like. For the Country version, chances are good that your tote won't be carrying a lot of weight, nor will it see a lot of abuse. If that's the case, a larger version probably won't need a stronger construction method than glue and nails.

For a hard-working version, though, consider reinforcing your tote at every joint and stress point. As I noted earlier, strengthening the attachment points of the handle is a good first step. Additional dowels to strengthen the bottom might also be in order if you plan to carry a lot of weight. More secure joinery at the corners, perhaps box joints or dovetails, might also be a good idea.

Consider, too, how you plan to use your tote. You might want to add compartments or dividers to keep tools or small parts separate, and for larger totes you might add a handy lift-out tray.

And if you don't like the alterations you've made, not to worry. This project is so easy to make you'll probably want to make more than one anyway.

HERE'S A BOX THAT MAKES A GREAT GIFT FOR the love of your life; you might even call it a gift from the heart. The first of three turned box projects in the book, I thought we'd start with this one as it involves only minimal lathe use. I've selected rosewood for this box, a dense and heavy species that is one of my favorite turning woods.

06 HEART BOX

Construction

Both the body of the box and the 1"-thick lid are created from the same workpiece, so the first step is to cut the workpiece into two components. The band saw is perfect for this (Fig 1). Take your time making this cut — the straighter you go, the less cleanup you'll have to do afterward. With what will be the lid cut free, mark one set of edges with registration marks so you can reorient it later for a smooth, continuous grain. Smooth the cut face of the lid. In Fig. 2 I've used my jointer, but a belt or disc sander will also do the smoothing quickly.

Transfer the heart pattern to both the lid and the main box body, being sure that you're keeping the grain oriented per your registration marks, and then attach a faceplate to the main body by your preferred method. I like to glue a piece of heavy paper to the back of the workpiece, and then glue that to the block screwed onto the faceplate, but you may favor a different method. Mount the workpiece onto the headstock of your lathe, as I've done in Fig. 3. You can see in this photo the arrow I've drawn onto it to serve as a registration mark for the lid.

REFERENCE	QUANTITY	PART	STOCK	THICKNESS	(mm)	WIDTH	(mm)	LENGTH	(mm)	COMMENTS
A	1	turning blank	rosewood	3	(76)	6	(152)	6	(152)	

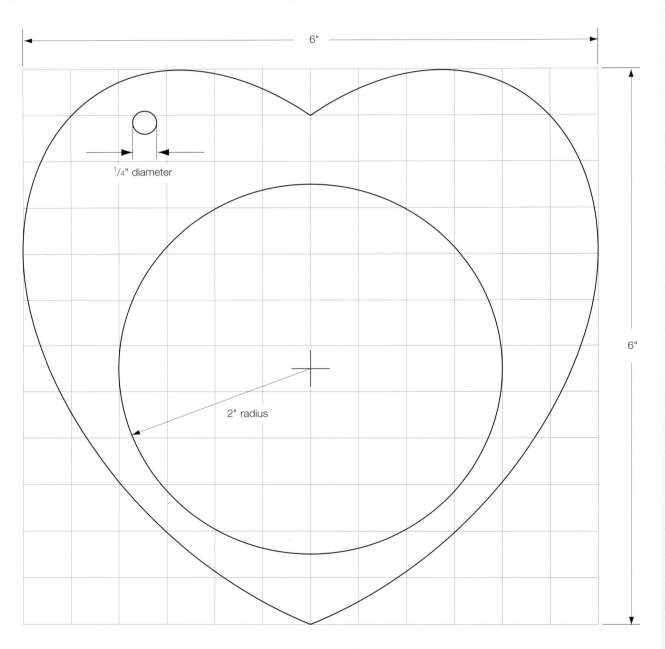

6"

6"

¹/₄" diameter

2" radius

Each square equals ¹/₂"

You probably also noticed that I've cut off the four corners to save time truing the blank on the lathe, which is a good start. I follow that up by using a heavy scraper to further true the turning blank, as in Fig. 4. This will make for a balanced turning and lower vibration. Take care not to take off too much of the corners or you might cut into the pattern.

Readjust your tool rest to the front of the workpiece to begin hollowing the box opening (Fig. 5). You can make this opening just about any diameter you like, but again take care not to get close to the heart pattern you drew on the front of the blank. Ideally, you want the thinnest point on the side walls to be no thinner than $\frac{1}{4}$". For the bottom of the box, I wouldn't go any thinner than $\frac{3}{16}$". In Fig. 6 I'm using a bevel gauge that I'd previously set to my desired depth. I can't stress enough that you should stop frequently to check the depth of the box opening; it's very easy to go too far, and cut right through the back of the blank, ruining the blank. Don't ask me how I know this.

When you're satisfied with the box opening, sand the front face and down inside the opening thoroughly while the workpiece spins on the lathe. Work your way up through finer grits, and you'll notice that as the grits get smaller and smaller, the workpiece will start to take on a nice shine. This is one of the things I love about extremely dense woods like rosewood: By using ever-finer grits of sandpaper, you can actually bring the wood surface to an attractive luster that sometimes requires no finish at all.

Remove the sanded workpiece from the lathe and faceplate, and orient the lid on top using your registration marks. Wrap strong packing tape around all four flat edges, and then cut out the heart pattern on the band saw as I'm doing in Fig. 7. It's OK to cut right through the packing tape, but you may need to stop and reapply a bit more to keep the two pieces oriented correctly until finishing the cut. The result is a heart-shaped box and lid that's exactly matched and with perfectly continuous grain (Fig. 8).

Pull out the packing tape again, but this time apply tightly to only one side of the heart, then head to the disc sander to smooth the lid and body simultaneously as in Fig. 9. Follow this up with ever-finer grits by hand or with a random orbit sander till you achieve a mirror finish on that side of the box assembly. With the first side done, remove the tape from the rough side, apply tape to the smooth side, and repeat the process.

With the second side sanded, leave the tape on a bit longer to keep the two pieces aligned for drilling the pivot point for the lid. I've elected to drill this 2"-deep hole on my drill press (Fig. 10). You can also use a handheld drill, but take extreme care to keep the hole perfectly vertical or the lid won't pivot correctly.

For the pivot, I used a ¼" steel rivet trimmed to just a hair under 2" long. Secure the rivet and lid by mixing a bit of epoxy and putting it in the hole in the box body. You won't need a lot, just a small amount will do, and be extremely careful not to get glue anywhere but in the hole. Slip the rivet through the lid, then place the lid onto the box and slide the rivet down into the epoxied hole. Once the glue has set the rivet will be frozen solid, allowing the lid to pivot freely.

I noted earlier that if you sand up through an extremely fine grit that no finish might be necessary and that's the case here. I've left the rosewood pretty much naked, applying only a bit of furniture polish.

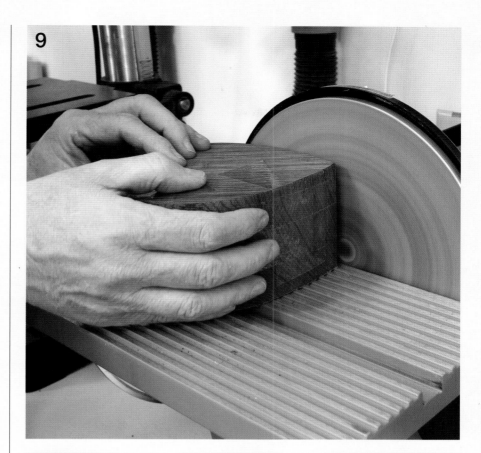

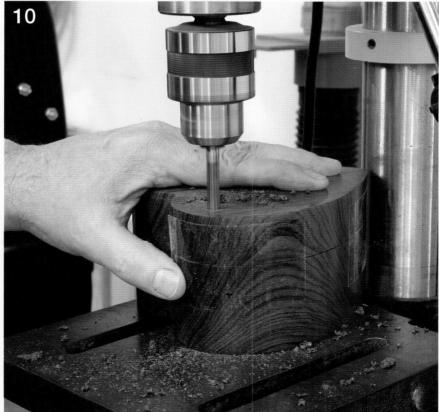

WORKING WITH WOOD CAN, DEPENDING ON the species, be a very aromatic experience. Pine, cedar, walnut and a host of other woods smell fantastic when they're being cut and shaped. But once the work is done and a finish applied to the wood, that lovely aroma all but disappears. This lathe-turned potpourri box is intended to smell good forever, and the open pewter lid allows whatever fragrance you choose to freely waft around your home.

I've made a lot of these boxes using a variety of hardwoods like cocobolo, zebrawood and purpleheart. However, I think my favorite for these is maple burl. Not only is burl highly stable when fully cured, which is ideal for a box that uses a metal lid, but I love the way the pattern changes as you work the wood — you literally never know what the final appearance is going to be like.

Because the opening of this box is turned to match the size of the metal potpourri cover, you'll want to order your covers before starting this project. These covers measure approximately 3" across which you'll need to match for the box opening, but you can size your turning blank as wide and as tall as you like. I prefer blanks that give a finished piece of about 4" wide and 4" tall, but feel free to vary this any way you wish — a very low, wide box would look nice as would a tall, narrow one, but whatever you choose remember that the opening size remains the same.

07 POTPOURRI BOX

Construction

With your potpourri covers in hand, this project starts just like the heart box by attaching a faceplate to your workpiece and mounting it to the lathe, followed by truing the workpiece to a perfectly round blank as in Fig. 1. This blank is about 4" long, not counting the faceplate and mounting block, so you'll notice that I've pulled in the tailstock to add support and steady the workpiece till I get it perfectly true and balanced.

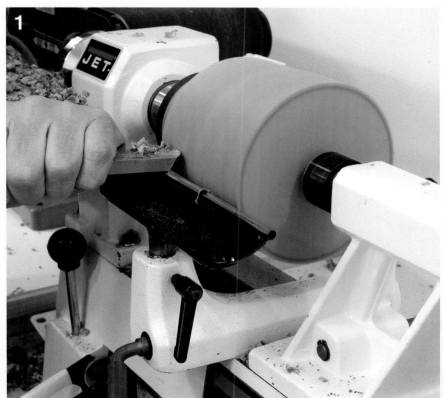

REFERENCE	QUANTITY	PART	STOCK	THICKNESS	(mm)	WIDTH	(mm)	LENGTH	(mm)
A	1	turning blank	maple burl	4	(102)	4¹/₂	(115)	4¹/₂	(115)
B	1	potpourri cover	pewter	3	(76)	diameter			

Pewter-finish potpourri cover —
Lee Valley Tools Ltd.
P.O. Box 1780
Ogdensburg, NY 13669-6780
1-800-871-8158
www.leevalley.com

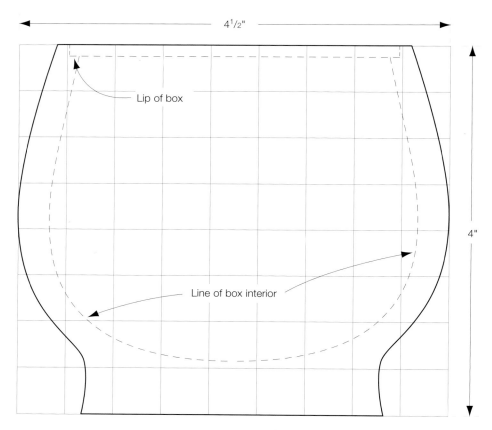

4¹/₂"

4"

Lip of box

Line of box interior

Each square equals ¹/₂"

2

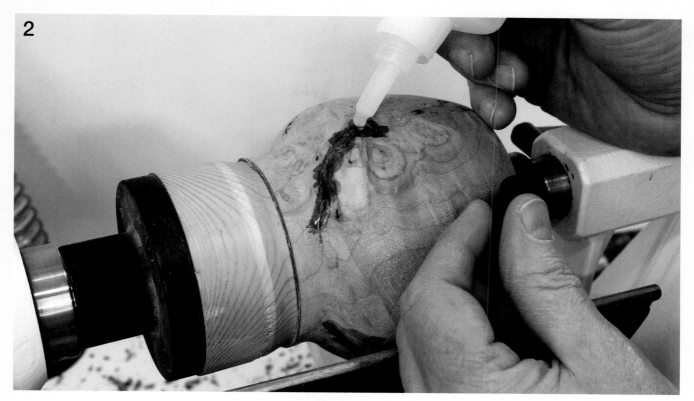

Turn the blank to whatever shape you desire. I've used a nice chunk of maple burl for the project box, which had a few voids and loose spots that appeared during turning. It's easy to stabilize these by drizzling a bit of cyanoacrylate or "super" glue into them as I'm doing in Fig. 2. Allow the glue to cure and finish the shape of your box.

As you're turning, be sure that the top is larger than the size of the cover. Remove the workpiece from the lathe temporarily and trace the cover on the top as in Fig. 3. This will act as your guide to sizing the top of the box and the style of the opening. You can do the opening two ways. The first, and easiest to do, is to leave the opening flat and plain — much like the lip of a coffee cup — and rest the pewter cover on top. (The covers have small metal studs on the underside that keep them in place.) You can see an example of this style of opening in the top photo on page 49. For the project box, I've elected to do the second style, which insets the metal cover down inside the opening a bit. To do this second style, you'll need to turn a small ledge — a circular rabbet joint, really — that the cover rests on.

3

Return the workpiece to the lathe and, using your traced outline of the cover as a guide, create the inset and rim of the ledge. No need to start going too deep into the workpiece yet, just enough that you can hold the cover in place to check for sizing as in Fig. 4. Stop and check the opening frequently as you work. You only get one shot at making the ledge and opening the right size: Go too far and the cover may end up falling down into the box.

When you're certain the lid opening and inner ledge are sized correctly, go ahead and hollow out the rest of the box. (Fig. 5) As with the heart box in the previous chapter, check the box depth frequently to avoid cutting through the bottom.

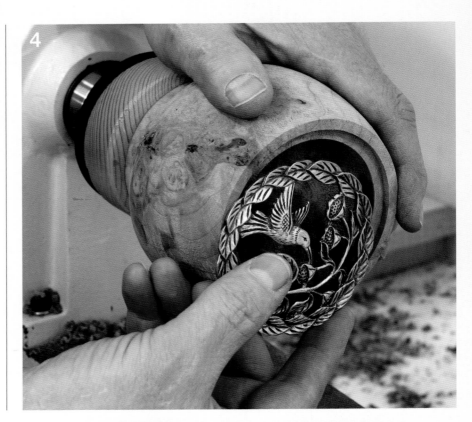

6

Sanding a perfectly symmetrical object on the lathe is a breeze — just set the workpiece turning and lightly move your sandpaper over the surface as it spins as in Fig. 6. Move through ever-finer grits to achieve the desired smoothness.

Finishing lathe projects is also easier, since you don't need to hold or touch the workpiece itself. Your finishing options are many here — you can choose a friction polish, French polish, a wiping varnish or even a classic finish of boiled linseed oil as I'm doing in Fig. 7. Simply dab the finish into the wood as you spin the workpiece by hand. When the finish cures, you can even rub it to a high sheen under power while still mounted on the lathe.

All that's left to do now is remove the finished box from the faceplate, and add your favorite potpourri.

7

FOR THE FINAL BOX IN OUR TRILOGY OF LATHE projects, we'll borrow a few characteristics from each of the previous two. Like the Heart Box, both the main box and lid come from a single workpiece in such a way that the grain runs continuously through both pieces. And like the Potpourri Box, the lid is formed in such a way that a portion fits inside the main box. Then we'll add a third element to make this Lidded Lathe Box stand on its own: a turned handle of exotic ebony.

Creating a box — or any project, turned on a lathe or otherwise — so that the grain forms a continuous run through all parts of the workpiece isn't easy. But it becomes particularly difficult on the lathe since you never know what directions the grain will go on the inside of the turning blank. You'll see what I mean as we progress here. Usually, though, you can count on at least one strong portion of grain or figure being dominant enough that it will continue in the turned workpiece.

08 LIDDED LATHE BOX

Construction

As always with a lathe project like this, the first steps are the same: Attach a faceplate to the workpiece, mount the blank on the lathe and turn it to a balanced uniform cylinder. In Fig. 1, I've already done that and I've started shaping the box. You'll notice that I'm using the tailstock to support the end of the turning. At this point, the workpiece is still mostly a spindle — and will remain so through the creation of the lid — so this support is necessary.

Keep turning until the workpiece has the overall shape of the complete box; that is, it should look pretty much the way it would with the lid in place. Decide the thickness you'd like the edge of the lid to be (I've chosen a ¼"-thick edge) and create a separation point with a parting chisel as in Fig. 2. Make this cut as deep as you want the lipped edge of lid to be; anything from around ⅛" to ¼" should work well. Once you've reached that depth, stop and move your parting chisel to the left about the same distance you've allowed for the depth of the lipped edge. Cut as deeply as you feel comfortable going, which will help to separate the lid from the main body of the box. You can't quite see it in Fig. 3, but I've left a ½" spindle down in that slot connecting the two pieces. That leaves enough to make the entire workpiece solid, but doesn't leave much to cut through to remove the lid.

REFERENCE	QUANTITY	PART	STOCK	THICKNESS	(mm)	WIDTH	(mm)	LENGTH	(mm)	COMMENTS
A	1	turning blank-box	spalted maple	4	(102)	5½	(140)	5½	(140)	
B	1	turning blank-handle	ebony	1	(25)	1	(25)	4	(102)	

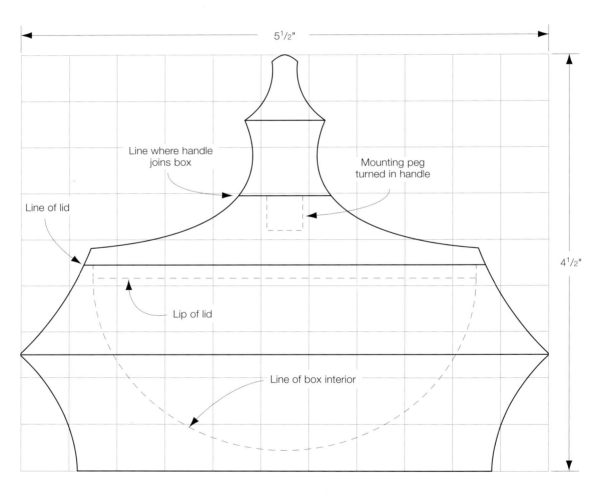

Line where handle joins box

Mounting peg turned in handle

Line of lid

Lip of lid

Line of box interior

5½"

4½"

Each square equals ½"

Removing the lid at this point is pretty easy. You can slip a saw down in that slot and cut through the connecting spindle to free the lid. (In truth, you really only have to saw part way through that connector to simply snap the lid off.) With the lid free, smooth the underside with a belt sander, random orbit sander or a hand-sanding block.

This next part is critical. Carefully measure the raised portion of the underside of the lid and transfer that measurement to the top of the main box, which should still be mounted on the lathe. A caliper helps significantly in this task, as in Fig. 4. When transferring this measurement to the main workpiece, it's a good idea to make it slightly undersized to give you a margin of error when turning the opening. You can always enlarge an opening that's slightly small; going the opposite direction, making a large opening smaller, well, not so much.

As we did in the Potpourri Box project, cut the opening in the main box, stopping and checking frequently for fit. At this point, don't start hollowing the box yet; only go deep enough to check the lid's fit. The perfect fit right now will be one that is very snug, which you'll want for the next step; final sanding later on will loosen that fit. When the opening is sized correctly to accept the lid, remount it on the workpiece and bring your tailstock back up into place, basically creating a single workpiece again. The first thing you'll notice is that the portion you cut away to create the lid has left an uneven edge on the box — you can see this in Fig. 5 — but that is easily leveled out by re-turning the outside of the box body until it flows smoothly into the lid.

With this completed, give the entire workpiece a thorough sanding (Fig. 6). You can see in this photo that I've flattened the top of the lid a bit where the handle will go. When the sanding is complete, use your parting chisel to remove the nub at the top of the lid, leaving a flat spot for the handle.

To prepare the lid for mounting the handle, in Fig. 7 I've installed a drill chuck in my lathe's tailstock to create a ³⁄₈" hole about ³⁄₈" deep into the top of the lid. (Lacking a drill chuck, you can do this on a drill press or with a hand drill.)

Finally, move the tailstock out of the way, remove the lid, and finish hollowing out the inside of the box. As with both previous projects, measure the depth frequently to avoid cutting through the bottom, and when the box is completely hollowed out to your satisfaction give it a good sanding on the inside, but don't yet do the final sanding of the inside edge of the opening. For now, we still want that lid to be snug.

6

7

Remove the workpiece from the lathe and install a spur center into the lathe headstock, then mount the turning blank for the handle. I've chosen ebony for this for a striking contrast to the light-colored maple, but you can use any species you'd like. Turn the workpiece to a uniform cylinder, then form the mounting peg that will go into the hole you drilled in the lid earlier. Again, a pair of calipers is your best bet to getting it sized correctly (Fig. 8). With the peg finished, take the entire workpiece off the lathe; we'll finish turning it shortly.

Cut off what was the headstock end of the spindle, leaving a ³⁄₈" peg, and glue the spindle into the top of the lid, pressing it down for a flush fit. Now, remove the spur center and return the entire box-lid-handle assembly to the lathe one last time. Turn the handle to shape, simultaneously forming the top of the lid for a smooth transition into the handle (Fig. 9), and follow with a full sanding of the outside. Use your parting tool to separate the lid at the top of the handle, then back off the tailstock and remove the box lid. With the project complete, the final step is to finish-sand the inside of the opening. Do this carefully; it's easy to over-sand, which might enlarge the opening too much. You want a nice, easy fit for the lid.

All that's left now is giving your lidded box a final finish. I chose an easy-to-apply wiping varnish, which I rubbed out to an even, satin sheen.

8

9

I NOTED AT THE OUTSET THAT BOXES ARE among the most popular projects woodworkers make as gifts, and that's the case with this one. My wife's side of the family is huge, so to make Christmas a bit easier everybody draws names for gift giving. A few years ago I drew my niece, Kim, and I designed the original version of this box for her. I had a supply of walnut on hand and a really nice piece of spalted maple, so I decided to make the box body out of walnut and top it off with a book-matched inset lid panel of the maple. I also wanted it to be a mitered box with a hinged lid, but beyond that I really wasn't sure what kind of design I wanted and so decided to simply wing it during construction.

I like heavy boxes and so I left the walnut its full thickness — about 7/8" — but was disappointed in

09 KIM'S CHRISTMAS BOX

the result about halfway through. It was plenty heavy and solid, but in spite of the wonderfully figured maple top it just looked too, well, "blah." That's when the idea for the angled sides hit me. I had plenty of thickness to work with, so I tilted my table saw blade and started running the box through, shaving off a bit at a time from the top and bottom until I liked the combination of angles. Kim's Christmas Box has always been one of my favorite projects, so for this book I decided to re-create it.

Construction

The book-matched panel is easy to create. Select a piece of figured maple (or any other wood) about ¾" thick that's a bit more than half the width of the panel you want, and resaw it carefully down the center, as in Fig. 1. This will give you two ⅜" pieces you can open up to reveal the figure mirror-imaged.

Now check the fit of the two edges, and if necessary, joint them for a perfect fit. Then just glue and clamp the two pieces up into your panel.

You can see in Fig. 2 that I'm making a couple panels — I only need one, but if I have enough stock I always try to make as many panels as I can, then save the rest for future projects. In fact, you'll see that second panel put to use later in Chapter 19. When the panel is dry, give it a few runs through a planer to smooth both faces and bring it to a final thickness of ¼".

REFERENCE	QUANTITY	PART	STOCK	THICKNESS	(mm)	WIDTH	(mm)	LENGTH	(mm)	COMMENTS
A	2	sides	walnut	$7/8$	(22)	$3 3/4$	(95)	11	(279)	
B	2	ends	walnut	$7/8$	(22)	$3 3/4$	(95)	5	(127)	
C	1	lid insert	spalted maple	$1/4$	(6)	4	(102)	$9 7/8$	(251)	
D	1	bottom insert	walnut	$1/4$	(6)	4	(102)	$9 7/8$	(251)	

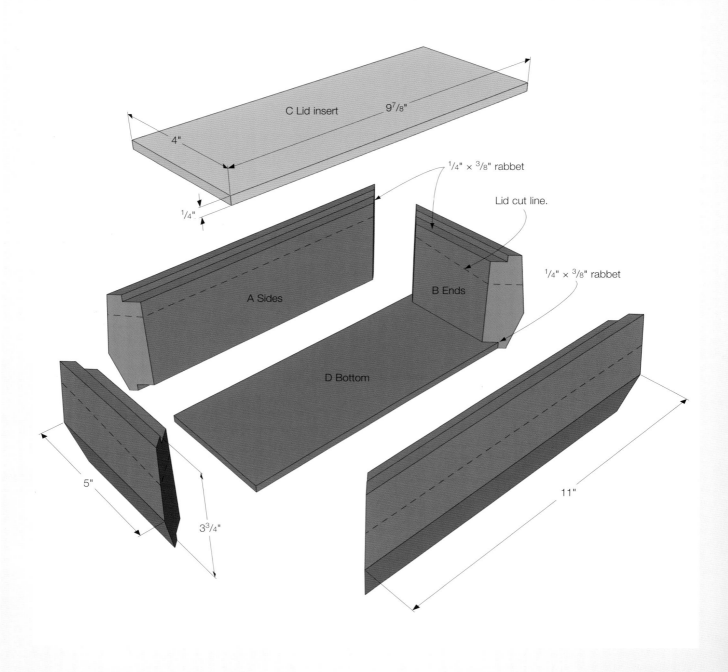

C Lid insert   9⁷/₈"

4"

¹/₄"

¹/₄" × ³/₈" rabbet

Lid cut line.

A Sides

B Ends

¹/₄" × ³/₈" rabbet

D Bottom

5"

3³/₄"

11"

Meanwhile, select and cut your walnut to width. If you want the grain to be nearly continuous, draw a diagonal mark from one end to the other to help keep the individual pieces oriented once you cut the two sides and two ends to length on the table saw. (Fig. 3) If you'd like, you can also number the sides to help keep them in order.

Now adjust your saw blade to 45° and miter the ends of all four pieces (Fig. 4). To make the rabbets for the inset lid and bottom panels, mount a dado head on your saw (or a straight bit in your router table), and mill a 3/8" wide by 1/4" deep rabbet on the top and bottom of the inside edges of each component as in Fig. 5. Glue and clamp up the box and allow to dry.

Now comes the tricky part. You'll want about ¼" of walnut around your inset panels after you've made your angled cuts, so mark the sides of the box at ⅜" from the end. This will be your "deadline" – you don't want to cut past it or you won't have enough of the walnut remaining to form a frame around the panels.

On the original version of Kim's box, I cut the angles in a trial-and-error way. But when done, the angles I liked best were 12° on the bottom and 5° at the top. The angles meet a bit less than 1½" from the bottom, giving the box a tapered, rising effect. You can see in Fig. 6 how these angles look when marked on the end of the box.

For that 12° angle on the bottom, set your blade to 78° and make the two end cuts using a miter gauge as in Fig. 7. Make these cuts slowly and carefully, because if you cut too deeply you won't get a second chance to make it right. It's perfectly OK to "sneak up" on your cut lines by taking multiple passes.

Cutting the sides is a bit easier, because you can use the endgrain from the cut ends as your guide. In Fig. 8, I've moistened the wood with a bit of mineral spirits so you can clearly see where the next cut should fall. Make the angled cuts on the side using your table saw fence (Fig. 9).

To cut the top angles, the procedure is the same, except this time set your blade at 85° to get the desired 5° angle on the top. As before, start by cutting the ends with your miter gauge, and follow by cutting the sides using the table saw fence.

Now install the lid and bottom panels. When dropping in panels, I like to bevel the leading edge a bit to allow room for the glue (Fig. 10). Apply glue to the rabbets at the top of the box, drop in the top and clamp it up till dry. As noted in an earlier project, always start with the top panel so you can reach in through the open bottom of the box and remove and glue squeeze out. The bottom isn't quite as critical, as any minor squeeze out will likely be covered up with an added lining in the bottom of the box. Still, you don't need to use gobs of glue here for these panels; a small amount works best.

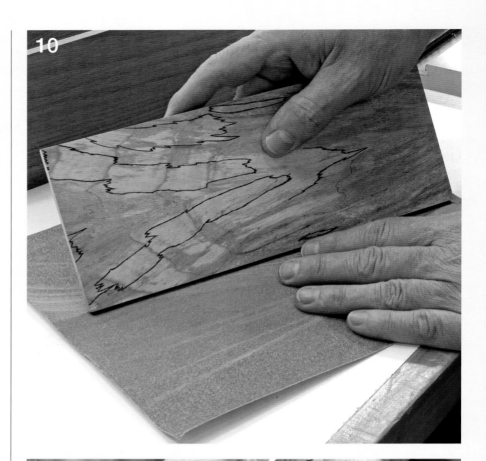

When both panels are dry, you can cut the lid free on the band saw as in Fig. 11. Because of the angled sides, the table saw isn't a good choice for this task. I wanted the lid to be angled, so there was no need to shim the box while cutting. However, decide before cutting which side of the box will be the front, as the cut should angle down toward the front. You'll achieve that cut by feeding the box through the blade on its back. Since we were careful to keep our components in order, you'll probably want the continuous grain in front. (When creating mitered boxes by keeping the cut parts in order, you'll get three corners with perfectly matched continuous grain; it's best to orient that fourth corner in the back where it won't be noticed.)

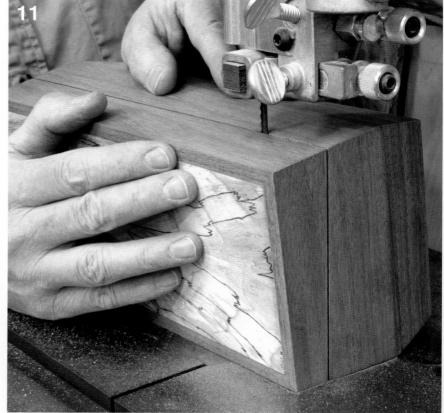

Now install the hinges of your choice. No-mortise hinges, as their name implies, require little preparation of the box and simply screw onto the rear edges. You'll see that kind of hinge used elsewhere in the book, but for Kim's box I chose to mortise in the hinges as in Fig. 12. Again, you have a choice here. For this box I've elected to mortise the hinge on the box body only, which is faster and easier, and makes no difference in how the lid operates. As you can see in Fig. 13, the finished mortise is deep enough to accept the entire hinge; the other leaf screws directly to the lid edge. Elsewhere in the book I'll install hinges with half-depth mortises cut into each side. The choice you use here is up to you.

For a finish I used several coats of satin polyurethane, which I rubbed out to a smooth sheen. On the inside is a piece of burgundy felt that, interestingly, is the only real difference between this re-creation of Kim's Christmas box and the original version I made several years ago: That one had green felt.

SOMETIMES I DON'T KEEP UP WITH TRENDS as well as I should (unless they have to do with woodworking, of course), but at some point during the last few years a type of decorative glass bead has become all the rage. With myriad designs and colors formed right inside the glass, the beads can be as unique as snowflakes. They're generally classified and grouped according to their main color, and they can be strung in any order or number on necklaces and bracelets. And because they're interchangeable, you can create a necklace that perfectly matches an outfit simply by swapping out beads.

By their nature, the beads are organized only when strung on a chain; between uses they have a tendency to rattle around inside jewelry boxes or other containers, meaning you have to dig and sift through to find what you want. This box puts an end to all that with its steel rods, perfect for hanging and lining up the beads in any order you want, and a glass top that lets everyone see and admire your collection — without touching them. I've chosen mahogany for this project, but as always you can substitute the wood of your choice. Also, feel free to adjust the dimensions as you wish to allow room for more, or fewer, bead rods.

10 BEAD BOX

Construction

We've covered mitered corners several times now — and there are two sets of miters in the Bead Box project — so I won't go into repetitive detail on those steps. Begin by cutting your four sides to length and width, and cut 45° miters on each end. This box is perfectly square, so all four sides are identical.

This box will have a ⅛" floating plywood bottom, which is installed into slots before forming and gluing the box shape. Cut these slots on the table saw as in Fig. 1. Set the blade at ³⁄₁₆" high, and lock down the fence ½" from the blade to place the slot correctly. Pass each of the sides over the blade to create the slot at the bottom edge. Since a standard table saw blade is ⅛" thick, the slot should fit your plywood perfectly. If you're using a thin-kerf blade you'll need to make two passes, adjusting the fence between passes to create a slot of ⅛".

Now cut the opening on the bottom edge of each side according to the provided pattern. I've cut the opening on the band saw as in Fig. 2, but a scroll saw would probably do a better job, and you can use a jigsaw in a pinch.

BEAD BOX • INCHES (MILLIMETERS)

REFERENCE	QUANTITY	PART	STOCK	THICKNESS	(mm)	WIDTH	(mm)	LENGTH	(mm)	COMMENTS
A	4	box sides	mahogany	3/8	(10)	2	(51)	6 5/8	(168)	
B	1	bottom panel	birch ply	1/8	(3)	6 1/4	(158)	6 1/4	(158)	
C	4	lid sides	mahogany	3/4	(19)	1	(25)	6 7/8	(180)	
D	2	rod supports	mahogany	1/4	(6)	1	(25)	5 7/8	(149)	
E	4	glass keepers	mahogany	3/16	(5)	1/4	(6)			sized to fit for length
F	1	glass	single strength	1/8	(3)	5 3/4	(146)	5 3/4	(146)	

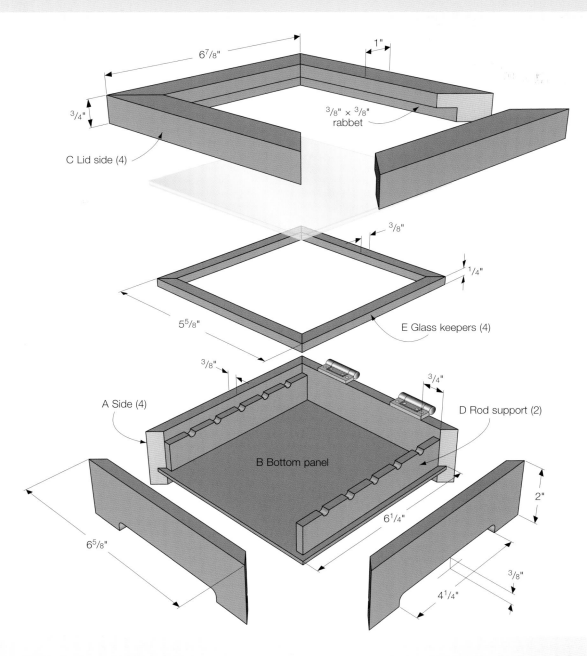

C Lid side (4)

6 7/8"

3/4"

1"

3/8" × 3/8" rabbet

3/8"

1/4"

5 5/8"

E Glass keepers (4)

3/8"

A Side (4)

3/4"

D Rod support (2)

B Bottom panel

2"

6 5/8"

6 1/4"

4 1/4"

3/8"

With all four openings cut out, smooth them on the spindle sander, or by hand (Fig. 3).

Tape up the backs of the miter joints and apply glue to the miters as we've done previously (Fig. 4). However, before folding the box closed slip the plywood bottom into place in one of the slots. Now just wrap the box around the plywood, clamp up the box and put it aside till the glue sets. Meantime, let's move on to the lid for some more mitering.

The most common joint used in picture frames is the miter joint, and that's appropriate here because with its clear glass insert that's exactly what the Bead Box lid is. Cut the ¾"-thick stock for the lid sides to its 1" width, but don't cut the parts to length or miter them yet. Set up a dado head in your table saw or a straight bit in your router table, and mill a ⅜" × ⅜" rabbet along one edge. This is much easier to do with a long piece of stock now, than it would be if you cut the lid pieces out first — they'd just be too short to handle safely when rabbeting. With the rabbet milled, cut the pieces to length and add a 45° miter to the ends as in Fig. 5.

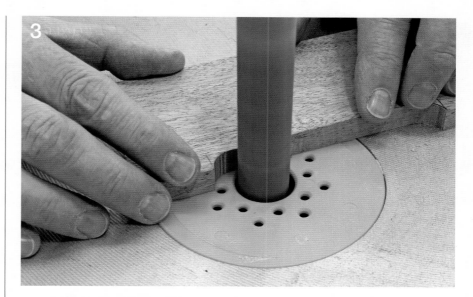

Once again, tape the backs of the miters and apply glue into the joints (Fig. 6). These parts are on the narrow side and the joints are small, which can lead to warping if you aren't careful. To help keep the lid frame flat and true throughout the glue-up, it's a good idea to tape, glue and form the lid frame on a dead-flat surface as in Fig. 7. Then check for square. (Fig. 8) When you're satisfied everything is flat and square, weigh down the lid frame as it dries to keep it flat on your assembly surface — I just set a heavy book on top of it and left it there till it was dry.

The rod supports require notches for the rods to rest in, and these must be evenly spaced on both sides of the box. This is easily done by cutting both support pieces and then taping them together on one side. Now mark your notch locations right across where the top edges meet, and with a ¼" bit drill holes right where the two pieces are butted together as in Fig. 9. You'll drill right through the tape on the underside; that's perfectly OK. When you remove the tape you'll have two pieces with perfectly matching half-holes along the top edge of each. Sand these pieces thoroughly, then glue and clamp them into the sides of the box. You can see from the lead photo in this chapter that I arranged mine so the rods and beads would be oriented side-to-side, but there's no reason you couldn't attach the rod supports so they'd be oriented vertically if you prefer.

Finally, attach the hinges. As always, you have a choice of hinge styles and I've opted for no-mortise hinges. These thin hinges have leaves that fit inside each other, meaning they don't create a big gap. As a result, you can mount your lid without mortising. This type of hinge isn't good for all boxes, but I think it works perfectly here. Mount the hinges on the rear edge of the box, and then use this trick to get your lid perfectly aligned. Tear some sections of double-stick tape and apply it to the edges of the hinge that attaches to the lid, as in Fig. 10. Now, carefully lay the lid in its exact position, and press down. Open the box and you'll find those hinge leaves stuck right where they belong. Use an awl to mark right through the tape in the hinge's screw holes. When you remove the taped-on lid you'll have the screw holes marked perfectly.

Finally, install a piece of single-strength glass into the lid frame opening with some ³⁄₁₆" × ¼" mahogany strips. (Fig. 11) It's often recommended that these strips be installed with small nails to facilitate glass removal, but I've rarely been able to drive nails into such a small frame without breaking the glass —

believe me, I've done it several times. And, on those occasions where I've successfully nailed the strips on, I've never found them to be particularly easy to remove if necessary.

Instead, I glue mine on, but use only the tiniest amount of glue. Just a small dot of glue on each end of the keeper strip, and one in the center. This is more than enough to hold securely, but the strips are easily removed if needed by slipping a utility knife behind the keeper strips and just popping them off.

There are a lot of options for customizing this box. I noted earlier that you can easily alter all the dimensions to make it larger or smaller, plus you can make additional notches to accommodate more hanger rods. I've designed this box with a plain plywood bottom with the intention of adding a lining, which I've done — you can see the results in the lead photo — but, if you prefer you can go with no lining, and instead install a matching mahogany bottom, or maybe something in a darker, contrasting wood species.

I wanted a bit of overhang on the lid so I've sized it slightly larger per the dimensions in the cut list, but you can make this lid flush if you want by adjusting the dimensions. You also don't have to use clear glass in the lid. Most of the projects I make for books and articles end up being given away, but when my wife saw me building this box she quickly claimed it for herself and requested a stained-glass lid insert instead of a clear one. You can see in the photo below how this box, now my wife's, turned out.

I'm thinking this probably means I'll be seeing a lot of receipts from the local jeweler fairly soon.

BACK IN THE DAYS BEFORE WALMARTS, malls, superstores, and a convenience store on every corner, people relied on the local general store for most of their shopping needs. From food and medicine, to hardware and domestics, they had pretty much everything. A prominent feature of every general store was a spool cabinet that could be found on a countertop near the fabrics and sewing needs. These cabinets usually had from two to six drawers (although some larger floor-standing units could have many more), each filled with row after row of spools of thread.

Those general stores are long gone, but the old spool cabinets pop up all the time at antique stores and online auction sites and they're quite handy for sewing enthusiasts and other crafters for storing supplies. My wife wanted one for years, but every one I could find was either too expensive or in really bad shape, or both, so I eventually made her one myself that exactly reproduced one of the three-drawer units. About a year later, I made her a mini cabinet just like this one that she could keep on her desk for storing pens, paperclips and other office supplies. It's such a fun project that I've re-created it for you here.

11 SPOOL CABINET

Construction

Don't be alarmed by the lengthy cut list; yeah, there are a lot of parts and numerous steps, but the construction is really pretty basic with mostly rabbet joints. Those frame-and-panel sides you see in the lead photo? Not to worry — they're fake and very easy to build.

In fact, let's start with those "paneled" sides. The side panels need to be ½" thick, but you'll make them by gluing ⅛"-thick faux frame pieces onto solid stock of ⅜". When you're done they'll look just like frame-and-panel construction. Don't worry about cross-grain gluing, these panels are so small that wood movement isn't an issue. Do the same for the box back.

Cut a long strip of ⅛" oak to 1¼" wide — you'll need nearly five feet of it altogether — and cut that into the lengths indicated on the cut list. Now, just glue them in place around the edges of the sides and back to imitate a framed panel as in Fig. 1. The longer pieces run vertically to mimic the "stiles," while the shorter pieces are placed in between to become the "rails."

With a dado set in your table saw or a straight bit in a router table, mill some ⅜" rabbets ¼" deep on the top, back and bottom edges of the end pieces as in Fig. 2. Without changing the setup, cut rabbets in the rear edges of the box top and bottom (Part "F"). Now, leaving the dado setup the same, adjust your fence to cut a dado exactly centered horizontally through the inside of each end panel to accept the center divider. Measure and locate this dado cut carefully — if you don't center it perfectly, your drawer compartments won't be the same size.

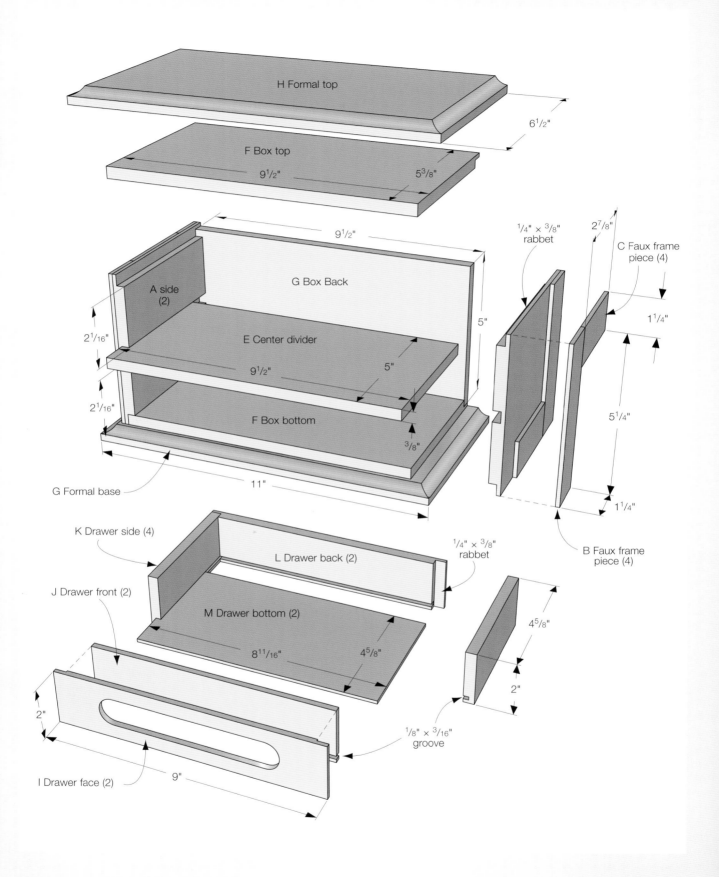

H Formal top

6 1/2"

F Box top

9 1/2" 5 3/8"

9 1/2"

A side (2)

G Box Back

2 1/16"

E Center divider

9 1/2" 5"

2 1/16"

F Box bottom

5"

3/8"

G Formal base

11"

1/4" × 3/8" rabbet

2 7/8"

C Faux frame piece (4)

1 1/4"

5 1/4"

1 1/4"

B Faux frame piece (4)

K Drawer side (4)

L Drawer back (2)

1/4" × 3/8" rabbet

J Drawer front (2)

M Drawer bottom (2)

4 5/8"

8 11/16" 4 5/8"

2"

2"

I Drawer face (2)

9"

1/8" × 3/16" groove

REFERENCE	QUANTITY	PART	STOCK	THICKNESS	(mm)	WIDTH	(mm)	LENGTH	(mm)	COMMENTS
A	2	sides	oak	$3/8$	(10)	$5^3/8$	(137)	$5^1/4$	(133)	$1/2$ thick with faux pieces
B	6	faux frame pieces	oak	$1/8$	(3)	$1^1/4$	(32)	$5^1/4$	(133)	
C	4	faux frame pieces	oak	$1/8$	(3)	$1^1/4$	(32)	$2^7/8$	(73)	
D	2	faux frame pieces	oak	$1/8$	(3)	$1^1/4$	(32)	7	(178)	
E	1	center divider	oak	$3/8$	(10)	5	(127)	$9^1/2$	(242)	
F	2	box top/bottom	oak	$3/8$	(10)	$5^3/8$	(137)	$9^1/2$	(242)	
G	1	box back	oak	$1/4$	(6)	$4^7/8$	(124)	$9^1/2$	(242)	$3/8$ thick with faux pieces
H	2	formal top/base	oak	$1/2$	(13)	$6^1/2$	(149)	11	(279)	
I	2	drawer faces	oak	$3/16$	(5)	2	(51)	9	(229)	
J	2	drawer fronts	oak	$3/16$	(5)	2	(51)	9	(229)	
K	4	drawer sides	poplar	$3/8$	(10)	2	(51)	$4^5/8$	(128)	
L	2	drawer backs	poplar	$3/8$	(10)	2	(51)	9	(229)	
M	2	drawer bottoms	birch ply	$1/8$	(3)	$4^5/8$	(128)	$8^{11}/16$	(220)	

Assemble the main box by spreading glue into the top and bottom rabbets in each side, and clamp up the assembly as in Fig. 3.

Check the box for square. In Fig. 4, I'm measuring the box from corner to corner — if the measurements are the same, the box is square.

When the assembly is dry, remove the clamps and temporarily drop the back panel into place. Now, slip the divider in through the front and reach inside with a pencil to mark an outline of where the divider will meet the back panel. Trim some masking tape to slightly narrower than the outline, and about an inch short of the ends of the back panel, and apply it inside the outline you drew as in Fig. 5. Why? Well, in a few moments we're going to stain the inside of the box before installing the divider — it's ridiculously difficult after the divider is in place — and that's where the divider will be glued. The tape will keep stain off that area.

Glue the back panel into place. You can see in Fig. 6 how I'm again using some scrap wood blocks as clamping cauls to evenly distribute the pressure.

Since we still have a lot of work to do we don't want to stain the outside yet, just the inside, so apply some masking tape along the front edges of the main box. Also put some tape on the ends of the divider so stain won't interfere with the glue when we install the divider later. Stain the divider and the inside of the main box, being careful to avoid those dadoes where the divider will go (Fig. 7). Allow the stain to penetrate for the amount of time recommended on the can, then wipe off all the excess. Oh, hey, here's another tip: Don't wear a white shirt when you're doing all this.

When the stain has dried, remove all the masking tape. Apply glue into the dadoes in the sides and on the back edge of the divider and slide it into place (Fig. 8). You don't need a lot of glue here; go sparingly to avoid excessive squeeze-out.

Let's put the main box aside for now and concentrate on the drawers. Like the panels, the drawer fronts are also made of multiple pieces face-glued to create a thicker workpiece. The drawer face is $3/16$" thick and has a centered cutout where you'll attach the labels, so start with these by cutting your drawer faces to width from material that's a bit longer — an inch or so on each end is good. (It's a good idea to copy, print and cut out the 1" × 6" labels on page 83 first, and then trace them on the stock for an exact opening.) Mark the correct length of 9" on these pieces, but leave them an inch or so longer on each end for now, to make them easier to work with, and you can trim them later. Tape these two pieces together on the ends, and trace the outline of the 1" × 6" labels in the exact center of the 9" face. Attached to each other, we can work them at the same time to create exactly matching cutouts.

Start the cutouts by using a Forstner bit to drill 1" holes at the ends of the

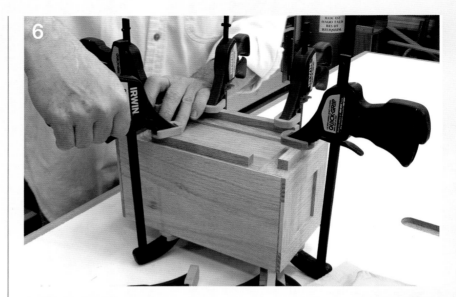

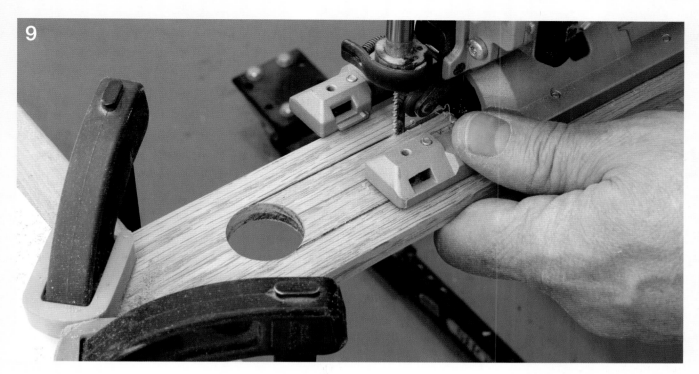

cutouts. I don't have a scrollsaw — man, I gotta get one of those — so in Fig. 9 I'm using my jigsaw to connect the holes along the lines to create the cutouts. Keep the two pieces taped together and smooth the opening on the spindle sander as in Fig. 10.

Now, trim the drawer faces to length on the table saw. In Fig. 11 you can see that I've removed the tape, but I've left the two pieces stacked to cut both at the same time. Give the opening a sanding on the front edges to round it over a bit.

Stack the drawer faces on the 3/16" drawer fronts and trace the opening in pencil. I like to outline that tracing in heavy black marker, as you can see in

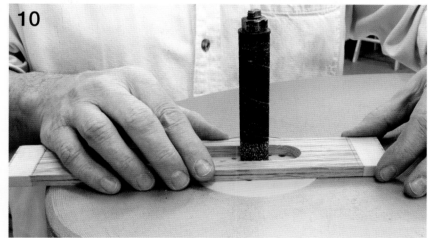

Fig. 12. This way, in case I trim the labels a little too narrow or short, the marker on the drawer front will fill the gap when I put the labels on. You don't want marker on the drawer faces, so set those aside when you do this.

Finally, glue the drawer faces to the drawer fronts, and clamp up till dry using a scrap block as a caul to evenly spread the pressure, (Fig. 13) and trim to final size if necessary.

Mill a ⅜" rabbet ¼" deep into the ends of the drawer front assemblies (on the back side) as in Fig. 14. Do the same for the drawer backs. Finally, remove the dado set

from your table saw and reinstall your regular blade, then cut a $\frac{1}{8}$" groove, $\frac{3}{16}$" deep around the bottom-inside edge of each of the drawer components. (Fig. 15) The groove should be about $\frac{1}{8}$" up from the bottom edge.

Start assembling the drawers by gluing the fronts into place. You'll note in Fig. 16 that I've temporary put the drawer backs in place "dry" to keep the glue-up square while clamping. When the glue on the drawer fronts has set, unclamp them and slip the drawer bottoms into place, (Fig. 17) then glue and clamp up the drawer backs. Check for square and allow to dry.

Let's see how you did. Unclamp the drawers and give them a test fit — a bit of tape to use as a temporary drawer pull is a good idea (Fig. 18). If

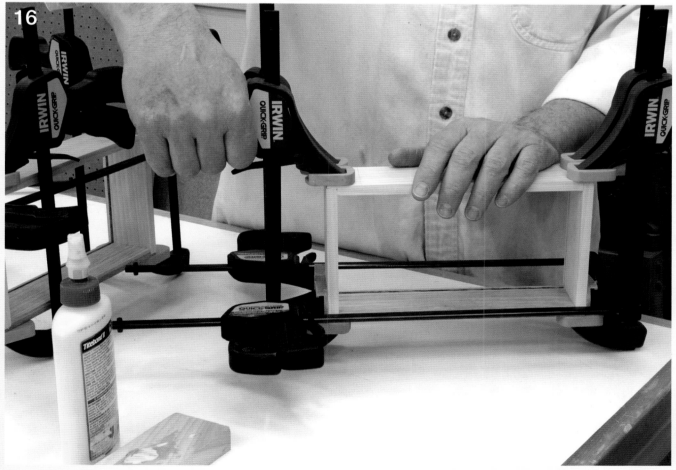

the drawer is too tight it could freeze in place and might be near impossible to get it out. I've said it before: don't ask me how I know this. If the drawers are too tight, you can sand the ends and/or tops on a belt sander, or shave off a narrow sliver on the sides on your table saw. Once you're satisfied that everything's a good fit, center and drill a hole halfway between the label opening and drawer end on the front of each drawer, centered top to bottom, for the drawer pulls.

Use your router table to mill an attractive edge profile around the circumference of both the base and formal top as in Fig. 19. I've elected to use a cove bit for the profile, but an ogee would also look nice. Glue and clamp the main box onto the base, (Fig. 20) then glue and clamp the formal top in place the same way.

Most of these spool cabinets were fairly dark, so I used a walnut stain on this one, but golden oak, mahogany or even a reddish cherry stain would also look good. Follow this up with the clear topcoat of your choice. I used polyurethane, but shellac would also be a good choice — most of the original old-time spool cabinets had a shellac finish, in fact — as would lacquer.

With the finishing done, all that's left is to attach the drawer pulls and labels. I've found that the labels work best when printed out on a matte or soft-gloss photo paper, which I then cover with a single layer of clear packing tape before cutting them out. If you've used an inkjet printer, this layer of clear tape will keep fingers or errant spills from smearing the ink over time. You can mount the labels in place with just about any kind of adhesive.

You can use your miniature spool box for just about anything, including sewing supplies of course. For the one I made my wife's desk, I installed dividers in the drawers to keep office supplies separated. Or, you can put felt linings in the drawer bottoms, if you prefer.

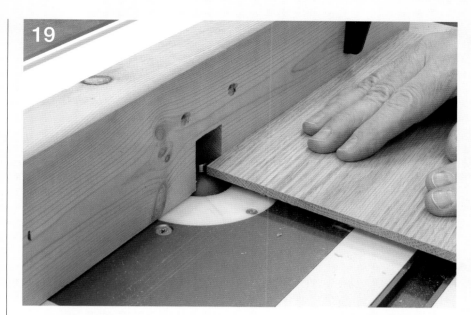

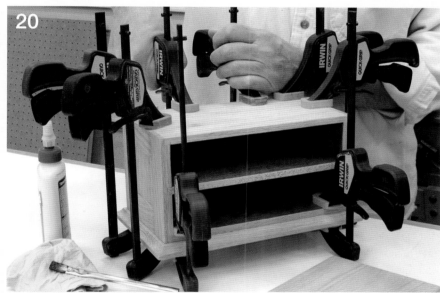

12 SHAKER OVAL BOX

WHEN IT COMES TO WOODWORKING, few styles include so many types of objects as Shaker design. From furniture to accessories to clocks to everyday household objects, if it was made of wood the Shakers seemed to have given serious thought to how it should look. With the possible exception of the straight, simple lines of their furniture, no objects exemplify the Shaker style more than their iconic bentwood storage containers.

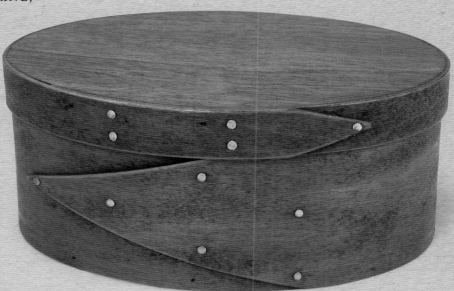

According to John Wilson, a Michigan woodworker and supplier who's been making Shaker boxes professionally for decades, the Shakers themselves never called them Shaker boxes, of course — that's a more recent term — but these delightful oval wooden boxes are so tied to Shaker culture that the name "Shaker box" is often applied generically to any bentwood box regardless of origin. In truth, bentwood boxes have been around for centuries in one form or another. Two main types are prominent today, with Shaker style being the most well known.

The other most commonly seen example is usually referred to as a "Colonial" box. Construction methods are the same as for Shaker boxes, wherein steamed or soaked wood bands are bent around a circular form with the box laps tacked into place. Except for slight variations in size and curve of the oval, the most notable difference is the shape and placement of the overlapping ends, called tails or simply laps.

Shaker boxes feature a series of multiple curved swallowtail "fingers" of varying number and width depending on box size. Wilson notes that although these fingers usually pointed to the right, a lot of folk believe that Shaker boxes always point to the right for religious reasons — a notion reinforced by the Internet — but numerous historical samples of left-pointing Shaker boxes exist. What is true about Shaker boxes is that the laps on both box and lid always point in the same direction.

Colonial boxes, like the one shown above overlap with a single point on the tail with straight edges. These can point either direction, but the laps on the box and the lid always point in opposite directions.

The sizing of Shaker boxes is described today by a numbering system that's fairly new — it's only been in common use for three or four decades — with larger numbers indicating larger boxes. This numbering system covers a huge range of box sizes. Wilson makes boxes from size #000 measuring a dainty 1" wide and 2" long, up to a #20 that comes in at about 26" × 38" — you could almost pack one for a week's vacation. The size of the box determines the thickness of the components. Wilson's #000 box uses bands as thin as .050" (about $^3/_{64}$"), while his #20 uses bands from .135" to .160" (around $^9/_{64}$" to $^5/_{32}$"). The inserts in the lid and box bottom vary correspondingly.

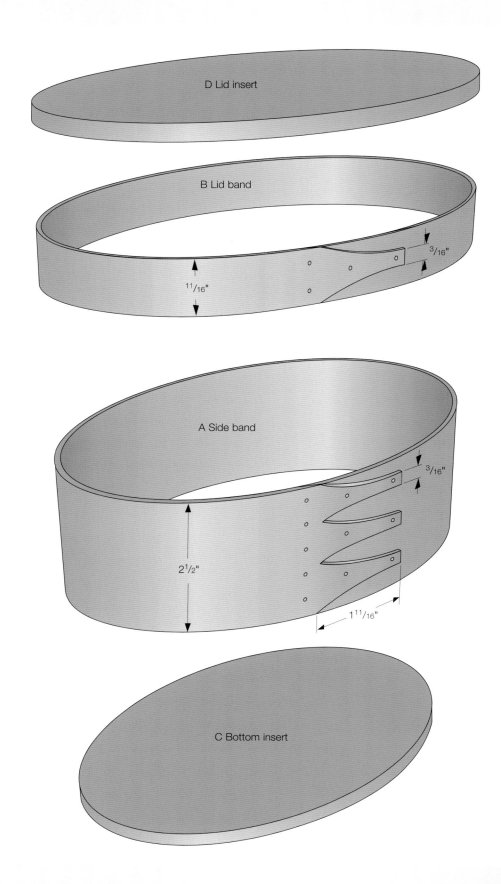

D Lid insert

B Lid band

$3/16"$

$11/16"$

A Side band

$3/16"$

$2^1/2"$

$1^{11}/16"$

C Bottom insert

SHAKER OVAL BOX • INCHES (MILLIMETERS)

REFERENCE	QUANTITY	PART	STOCK	THICKNESS	(mm)	WIDTH	(mm)	LENGTH	(mm)	COMMENTS
A	1	side band	cherry	$1/16$	(2)	$2 1/2$	(64)	23	(584)	
B	1	lid band	cherry	$1/16$	(2)	$11/16$	(17)	24	(610)	
C	1	bottom insert	cherry (quartersawn)	$1/4$	(6)	$4 1/2$	(115)	7	(178)	
D	1	lid insert	cherry (quartersawn)	$1/4$	(6)	$4 11/16$	(119)	$7 1/8$	(181)	

Additonal Supplies: $3/16$" copper tacks; toothpicks.

Comments: Overall dimensions reflect width and length of finished lid. Measurements shown for the Lid Insert (Part D) are approximate, and determined by final dimensions of the main box body after bending, tacking and shaping.

SOURCE LIST

John Wilson & Eric Pintar, LLC
406 E. Broadway
Charlotte, MI 48813
(517)543-5325
www.shakerovalbox.com

Wilson carries all materials for making Shaker boxes, including forms and patterns, hardwood bands, lid/bottom inserts, tacks and soaking trays.

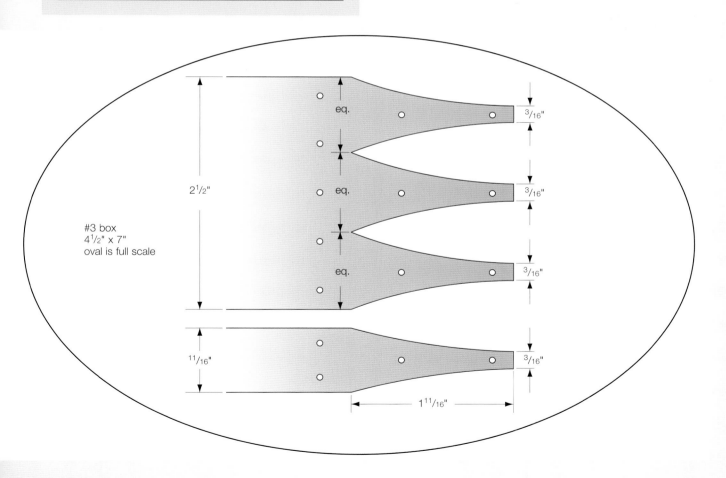

#3 box
$4 1/2$" x 7"
oval is full scale

Notes on Shaker Boxes

Unlike most of the projects in this book, before you can build a Shaker box you'll need some very specific supplies and a few shop-made jigs. Let's take a look at what you'll need.

Wood

The bands that take on the bent shape are quite thin as noted earlier. Some of the most common sizes of boxes use stock of around $1/16"$ or less, which can be difficult to make in the shop. Planing woods to this thickness can be difficult and even dangerous — anything less than $1/8"$ thick can break apart during planing, sending shards into the cutter-

head like shrapnel. Danger aside, the results of planing that thin aren't always optimal. While the box lid and bottom inserts are of thicknesses easily milled in the shop, it's best to purchase bending stock from a woodworking supplier.

Water Bath

Wood softens enough for bending when bathed in hot water (or steam). The ideal water bath is a long metal tray roughly the shape and size of a window box liner or one of those wallpapering trays. A few decades ago metal versions of those were easy to come by, but these days they're all plastic. You can still find these at flea markets and through some specialty suppliers. However, you can also use an ordinary roasting pan, as I'll do later in the project. Roasting pans are too short to lay the wood bands right in the water, so you'll need to introduce the bands slowly into the hot liquid by dipping half in first and allowing it to soften, then bending it down into the water (pretty much like you would when cooking long pasta).

You can always heat the water on the kitchen stove and do your bending in there, but in the shop you can use a hot-plate or small gas grill (never use a charcoal grill indoors). You don't want the water boiling. A temperature around 180 degrees is good, but don't fuss too much over thermometers and such. As long as the water is good and hot, your wood will bend just fine.

Forms and Shapers

To achieve a precise shape, bending wood requires something on which to shape it. Shaker boxes use two items to achieve this. The first is a bending form sometimes called a "core." (photo, opposite, bottom). This is a solid block of wood around which the bands are initially bent to achieve an approximate shape and, more importantly, the correct size for locating the lap locations. These bending forms are cut in the exact shape and size of the box interior; their height is at least that of the band height. You can make these out of any wood you have lying around, gluing multiple pieces to achieve the correct height.

Once the laps have been tacked securely into place and the box size locked in, and while the wood is still wet and

pliable, shapers like those shown in the photo above are pushed into the lid and bottom of the box to hold it till dry. Holes in the shapers allow airflow. Again, these can be made of any wood. Their overall sized is just slightly larger than the cores, but the edges receive a bevel of 10 degrees and they're inserted like corks into the tacked bands.

Tacks

The Shakers typically used copper tacks, although a number of historical samples evidence steel tacks. These tacks are clinched over on the inside of the box and so their length should be about $1/16$" more than the box where the bands overlap. For example, a box using bands of $1/16$" would need to be $3/16$" in length.

Anvil

For clinching tacks, an anvil provides a solid metal backing that forces the tips of the tacks over and back into the wood as they're driven, holding it securely. This anvil isn't fancy, and can consist of any short length of pipe held in a cradle of some sort. You can see mine in the photo at left. It's a pipe borrowed from one of my clamps, and it rests in open slots on a pair of upright lengths of 2×4 attached to a 2×4 base. Alternatively, if you have a solid bench vise you can clamp the pipe there.

Construction

For this project I've elected to do a #3 box because it's a good size for gifting and household use and a perfect size to work with — not so small that bending and tacking are difficult, and no so large as to be unwieldy. Also, the #3 box uses $1/16$" cherry stock for the bands; although it can be a difficult thickness to plane down to in the shop, it's readily available from most woodworking suppliers.

Begin by heating your water. It may take a while to get the water hot, so start it going now while you prepare your working components.

Cut the bands for the main box and lid to size, then transfer the finger patterns to the ends of each. You can cut these fingers with a band saw, but a fine-cut blade is a must, and unless you have a zero-clearance insert in your band saw table you may get a lot of tear-out on the underside of these delicate fingers. I opted for a very sharp utility knife, as you can see in Fig. 1. Use fine sandpaper to smooth the finger edges after cutting. Add a bit of a bevel to the top edges of the fingers with the knife or sandpaper. This bevel shouldn't be large, no more than 10°.

Now, drill pilot holes per the pattern locations with a $1/16$" bit. (Fig. 2) This will prevent splitting in the narrow fingers when driving the tacks later.

Since the bands wrap over on top of themselves when bending the box and lid to shape, you want a smooth transition on the inside of the box which you can achieve by feathering a long bevel — about 1-1-/2" to 2" — where the ends of the bands contact the inner surface of the box and lid. Not only does this look better, but it helps ensure a smooth fit when inserting the lid and bottom inserts. Keep in mind that this feathered bevel faces outward, so do it on the same side of the bands that you beveled the fingers. You can do the feathering by hand with a sanding block, but applying the ends with even pressure to a belt sander accomplishes the feathering quickly and evenly. (Fig. 3)

With the two bands prepared, it's time to start "cooking." If you're using a long tray you can just drop the bands in. I'm using a large roasting pan, and in Fig. 4, you can see how I've softened the first portions of the band a bit, then curled it so it can slip into the water around the circumference of the pan. Let the bands soak for 10 to 20 minutes in the hot water.

Start the shaping with the main box band. Use tongs to remove the band, and then wrap it around the #3 bending form as in Fig. 5, making sure that the feathered end and beveled edges of the fingers are facing outward. You need to work quickly because the band will cool pretty fast, but don't panic — if you don't get it quite right, you can put the band back in the water and try again. (It will bend a bit more easily the second try.) Pay particular attention in this photo to how I'm using my thumb to hold all three of the band fingers at the same time as I wrap the band around the bending form. By holding all three evenly, it helps prevent the wood from splitting between the fingers.

When you have the band securely in place around the form, mark the band in a couple spots, as in Fig. 6. You'll have to take

the band off the form to tack it, and will need these marks as a guide to reforming the circular shape on the anvil. When you have the band marked, take it off the form. Now that the wood has cooled, you'll notice that although it pops right out of its oval shape that it's still plenty bent.

Before proceeding further, this is a good time to put the lid band into the hot water so it can be softening up while you move through the next few steps.

Using your marks, bend the band around your anvil — the shape will be more circular at this point than oval, but that's OK for now; we'll get it into its correct shape shortly. Hold the band securely and begin tacking through your pilot holes one-by-one as in Fig. 7. By nailing right on the pipe, the portion of the tack that comes through the inside of the box (about 1/16") is immediately clinched over as you tap it home.

Remove the fully tacked band from the anvil. Although it's cooled considerably, it's still plenty pliable. This is where the shapers come in. Insert a shaper into the top like a cork and push it down into place as in I'm doing in Fig. 8. You'll immediately see the band take on its correct oval shape. Rotate the shaper as needed to adjust the oval so the tacks are

near the center of the box side. Depending on how you've cut and beveled your shapers they may or may not fit all the way down in with moderate pressure, and that's fine. You only want them to be a bit snug; don't pound them in place so tightly that you end up creating a bevel at the top. My #3 shapers are a bit on the small side, and although they fit completely inside the box they're not that tight. Now flip the box over and insert the other shaper into the bottom.

Flip the box right side up. Use tongs to get the lid band from the hot water bath and wrap in around the top of the box as in Fig. 9. (Again, be sure the beveled edges of the finger face outward.) Make some guide marks on the lid band as you did before. Remove it from the box and head over to your anvil, and tack the finger as you did for the main box band.

Slip the finished lid band over the top of the box, being sure to align the tacks. (Fig. 10) Again, my shaper fits down inside my box, but if yours protrudes cork-like from the top of the box, you may need to temporarily remove the shaper to slip the lid band into position. Replace the shaper when you have the lid band on.

That's about all you can do with the box for now, as it needs to dry thoroughly so it will rigidly remain in a perfect oval when the shapers are removed. Give the box at least 24 hours to dry; it's best to lay the box on its side so air can move freely though the holes in the shapers. Don't try to rush things by heating it or putting in the sun or it could dry too quickly, which can cause warping and cracking. Check to see how it's doing after a day — if it still feels damp, give it some more time, maybe even another 24 hours. Remember that the top of the box is a double thickness of wood where the lid band wraps around, and that portion will take the longest to dry.

While the box is drying, prepare your stock for the lid and bottom inserts. Because these boxes are very light and thin, they can be greatly affected by wood movement. The bands aren't an issue as they're not "captured" across their width, but the inserts are. For that reason, using quartersawn wood is best as its seasonal movement is far less than flatsawn stock.

After the box and band are thoroughly dry, remove the shapers. Set the main band on your ¼" stock for the box bottom and trace around the inside of the box. (Fig. 11) The box should be pretty stable at this point, but avoid flexing it as your trace or you could alter its shape. Repeat the process for the lid band, and keep in mind that the lid insert will be slightly larger than the one for the bottom because the lid band encircles the outside of the box.

When tracing the bands for the lid and bottom insert, be sure to mark the portion that goes next to the laps. Due to the overlapping wood on that side, the inserts may not be perfectly symmetrical. This is especially true of the lid insert. The overlapping portion of the lid band is right over the lapped band on the main box. This means that at that location on the box, there's a double thickness of wood that must be taken into account — the lid insert will "bulge" very slightly at this spot. By marking the lap location, you can be sure to orient the lid insert the right way.

Cut out the two inserts on the band saw as in Fig. 12, but don't cut all the way to the line. We're going to fine-tune and smooth the oval curve, plus put a bit of a bevel on the edges of the inserts.

As with the shapers, the bottom and lid inserts receive a slight bevel that imparts a cork-like clamping action that tightens the inserts as they're pushed fully into place. This bevel isn't as large as the 10° bevel on the shapers; a bevel of no more than 3° or 4° is good. Making these bevels is a bit tricky — remember that we traced the inserts from the inside of box and lid bands, so you can't just tilt the table on your disk sander down 3° or 4° and sand up to the line or the bevel will be on the wrong side. Instead, tilt the sander table up 3° or 4°. Most sanders have a positive stop at 90° to the disk, so you'll need to defeat this in some manner; usually just removing the angle-set knob and holding the table at the desired upward angle with a clamp does the trick. (Fig. 13) Sand up to your traced lines.

When mounting the inserts into the box and lid, pay attention to the orientation, as it's easy to lose track with all this flipping the box and lid over. As noted earlier, it doesn't matter which way the fingers point, but they must point the same direction on both lid and box to keep with Shaker practice. Also, keep in mind that the process involves more than a little trial and error. You want a snug fit, but if you're struggling to get the inserts into the bands, head back to the sander to remove a bit more stock around the edge. Do this extremely carefully and slowly. You want to sneak up on a good fit; sand too much and a too-loose insert becomes scrap and you'll have to start over.

This is where you'd normally reach for your glue bottle,

but don't; no glue needed. Slip the lap edge into the box opening first, so as not to snag on the inside feathered lap, as in Fig. 14. Gently press the insert into place all the way around. Again, if this requires an inordinate amount of force — or if one problematic spot seems to snag on the way in — sand a bit more till the fit is snug but not a struggle. Press the inserts in until they're flush with the bands.

To anchor the inserts, the Shakers used wooden pegs. Drill a series of $1/16"$ holes every few inches around the perimeter of the box and lid inserts, as in Fig. 15. For a #3 box, I usually space the holes every 2" to $2\frac{1}{2}$"; for larger

boxes a wider spacing is acceptable. These holes don't need to be deep. Again, for a #3 box a depth of ⅜" to ½" is fine.

Slip lengths of toothpicks into the holes — again, no glue needed — and tap them solidly home with a light hammer. Clip the toothpicks off just above the surface. (Fig. 16). Sand all the pegs flush with the surface of the bands. Sand the lid and bottom so the inserts are flush with the edges of the bands — you can do this on a belt sander if you wish, but remember that these boxes are thin and light, so sand gently and slowly — then give the entire box a good sanding inside and out by hand, working up through the grits till you get a smooth surface. Take care sanding around the fingers, as it's easy to snag sandpaper under them.

For a final finish, you have a few options. You can paint the outside of the box (that's what the Shakers usually did until the mid-19th century) or apply a clear coat of shellac, varnish or other oil. I gave the project box several coats of boiled linseed oil, rubbed out to a soft sheen. However, for a box that may get a lot of rough use, especially near a kitchen or bathroom sink, polyurethane is a good choice.

ASK ANY WOODWORKER WHAT THE MOST versatile tool in the shop is and you're guaranteed to create a heated discussion. For me, the question has always been an easy one: It's the band saw. A band saw's abilities are limited to cutting, of course, but it can make just about any kind of cut any other saw can. You can both rip and do crosscuts, like on a table saw. Also like a table saw you can resaw stock, but in much wider capacities and with a smaller kerf for less waste. For quick cutoff chores, I find my band saw faster and less trouble than setting up either my miter saw or table saw.

But its real value is cutting curves. Sure, a jigsaw can do that, but a band saw handles thicker stock, and makes cleaner cuts no jigsaw can match. And when it comes to making intricate curves that can be reassembled with almost no hint of a cut line, you won't find another cutting tool that does a better job.

I've used a band saw several times throughout this book, but mostly for its basic cutting ability. But

13 BAND SAW BOX

for this project, the band saw can create every bit of stock needed for a beautiful box from a single block of wood as well as create the curved interior. Once assembled, the box will have almost-invisible joints, and the grain will flow smoothly across the entire surface.

You've probably seen band saw boxes that are intricately shaped with continuous grain, and flowing curves as the dominant feature. I like those and have made them before, but for this project I wanted to create something with very straight lines but still with that continuous grain. And since the wood I'd selected for this project — a slab of spalted maple burl — I wanted the grain to be dominant, not the curves.

Construction

I love working with burl. It's a very stable material when well seasoned that's adaptable to oddly shaped work, and its no-two-are-like uniqueness can't be beat. Add the contrasting swirls of spalting and the beauty is unmatched even before you start working with it. However, spalting (which is created by a wood fungus) can lead to softness in areas of even the hardest wood — it can give the wood a "punky" consistency — so chose carefully. In Fig. 1, you can see how I've cut my workpiece from an area of the burl near the edges of the spalting. The wood is strongest here, plus I like how the spalting is delineated in the center of the workpiece as it blends into the non-spalted portions.

When you've cut out your workpiece, thoroughly square it up. The jointer works well for this (Fig. 2). Once square and true, give the workpiece a good sanding — remember this is what your finished box will look like, so now's the time to make sure you're pleased with the overall workpiece itself before cutting it into your working components.

Building a band saw box is a process of first disassembling the main workpiece. Begin by slicing off the two box sides, as in Fig. 3. The

BAND SAW BOX • INCHES (MILLIMETERS)

REFERENCE	QUANTITY	PART	STOCK	THICKNESS	(mm)	WIDTH	(mm)	LENGTH	(mm)	COMMENTS
A	2	sides	spalted maple burl	3/8	(10)	2 1/2	(64)	7 1/2	(191)	A, B & C are cut from single block
B	1	bottom	spalted maple burl	1 5/8	(41)	3	(76)	7 1/2	(191)	Thickness is overall height.
C	1	top	spalted maple burl	7/8	(22)	3	(76)	7 1/2	(191)	Thickness is overall height.
D	2	lid keepers	ebony	1/4	(6)	1 1/8	(29)	1 1/2	(38)	
E	1	lift handle	ebony	3/8	(10)	3/4	(19)	2 1/4	(57)	

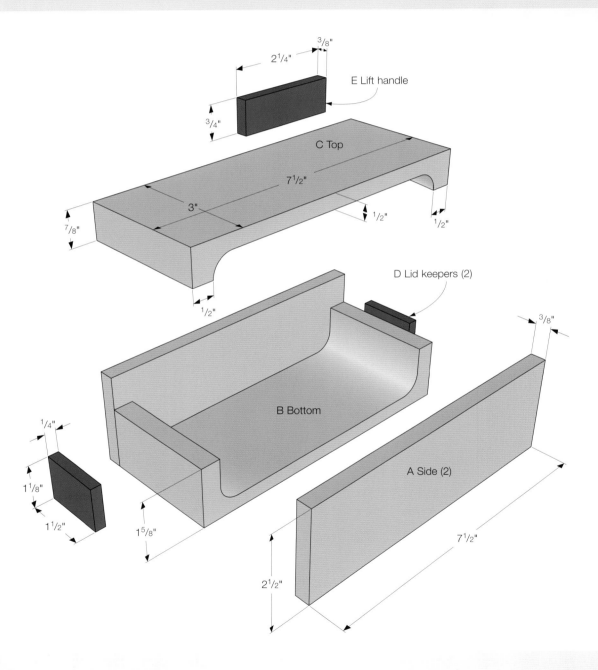

E Lift handle

C Top

D Lid keepers (2)

B Bottom

A Side (2)

value of the band saw becomes apparent immediately with these first cuts: The kerf is so thin, the grain and spalting patterns are largely uninterrupted. Make these cuts slowly and carefully — you want them as straight as possible so as not to enlarge the kerf when cleaning up the cut faces. I installed a new blade just before starting this project, so my cuts were already pretty clean, but it's still necessary to completely flatten and smooth the mating surfaces. Do this carefully and slowly, too; you want to remove only as much material as needed for a smooth face. For the flattest sanding possible, note that in Fig. 4 I'm sliding the pieces on a

full sheet of sandpaper on the flattest spot in my shop, the cast iron wing of my table saw. With the inside faces of the sides smooth, do the same to exposed faces of the cutout center portion.

Transfer the cutout pattern to the sides of the center portion. This cutout forms the box interior, and when separated will create both the box lid and bottom. Begin the cut by slicing straight through the center on the lid lines on each end to make two easier-to-handle workpieces, and then cut out the waste (Fig. 5). In Fig. 6 you can see how these cuts compare when complete. You can see a bit of burning on

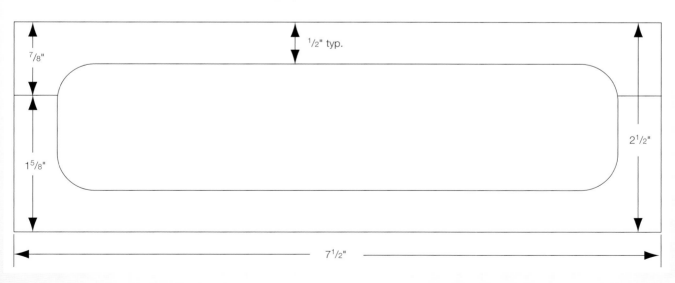

5

the wood surface in this photo. Maple is very hard, and making slow cuts through it — especially curved cuts — can do this. Not to worry, we'll remove this shortly. I should note here, too, that I referred to this center cutout portion earlier as "waste." I misspoke. There's really no such thing as waste or scrap in my shop. That thin cutout portion will eventually adorn a small drawer front on a future project, while that thicker portion is the perfect size for a set of spalted-burl wine stoppers.

Now, let's clean up the rough inner surface created when cutting out the center. Temporarily reassemble the two pieces with packing tape, probably the second most-useful tool in the shop after the band saw. (Fig. 7) With the pieces connected, head to the spindle sander to smooth out what will be the inside surfaces of the box as in Fig. 8. When done, separate the two pieces and give each a thorough sanding on the inside curved surface by hand with increasingly finer grits of sandpaper. Remember that this is the box interior and it's now essentially complete, so this step is actually finish sanding.

6

7

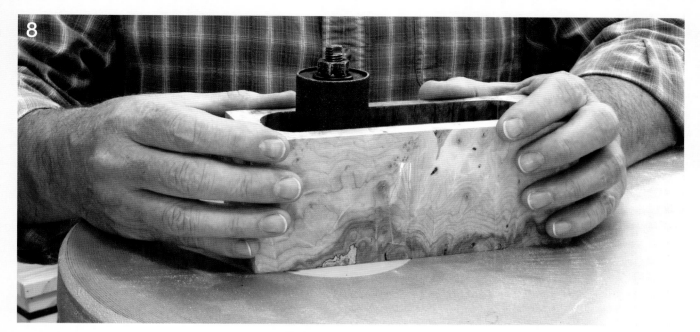

Here comes the fun part, reassembling the box. Apply glue to the edges of the lower portion of the inner piece, and glue the sides back on. Line everything up carefully and clamp up the assembly till dry. (Fig. 9) It's important when clamping that you watch the workpieces carefully to be sure they don't slide out of alignment. Although slight movement could easily be fixed when we sand the exterior of the box later, any slipping will ruin the continuous flow of the grain and spalting. If you notice any slipping at all, correct it now and reseat the clamps.

When the box is dry, put on the lid and secure it with packing tape. No matter how well the glue-up went, you'll still need to smooth those glue joints to help them disappear. This is easily done by sanding the ends of the box on the disc sander as I'm doing in Fig. 10, or with hand sanding. Do the same on the underside of the box, although I recommend doing this the same way we did the sides earlier, with a sheet of sandpaper on the table saw wing to ensure a perfectly flat bottom. Finally, do a thorough hand sanding of the entire

outside of the box with increasing grits. Maple burl sands very smooth, and when done carefully you can achieve a glasslike surface even before applying any kind of finish.

To make the lid keepers and handle, cut a few rectangles of ebony to the dimensions on the Cut List, and give them a thorough sanding. (Fig. 11) Ebony shines up beautifully when sanded to high grits, and in this photo I've started with 400-grit, moved up to 600 and finished with 800. Even before assembly, those pieces gleam.

Ebony sometimes doesn't take regular woodworking glues well, so we'll attach these pieces with epoxy. Score the gluing surface on both the ebony and the box itself before applying the glue, which will add some mechanical strength to the glue bond. In Fig. 12, I'm using the tip of a small utility knife to scratch grid lines into the glue surface. Glue the pieces in place until the epoxy cures, securing them with clamps as needed. (Fig. 13)

Those lid keepers won't experience much stress, plus they have a fairly large gluing area for their size

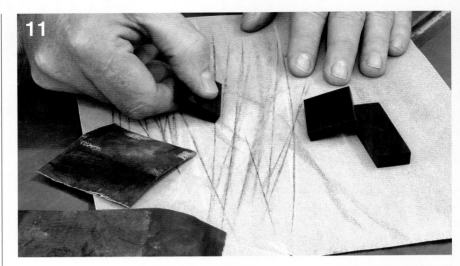

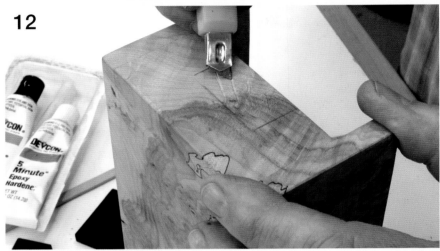

so those won't need any reinforcement. That's just the opposite for the lift handle, though, which has only a narrow edge for gluing. Strengthen it by drilling a pair of ⅛" holes up into the handle from the underside of the lid. Epoxy short lengths of hardwood dowel into the holes, then trim them flush on the underside when the glue cures, as in Fig. 14. Sand the dowels smooth.

The hardness of maple burl means that it doesn't need a lot of protection when it comes to a final finish, plus sanding to high grits already gave it a bit of sheen, so a plain boiled linseed oil finish might be a good choice. I wanted just a bit more shine, so I've chosen a tung oil finish. As you can see in Fig. 15, when the oil hits the surface the exquisite burl figuring almost literally explodes out of the wood. It's easy to see why burl is a favorite choice to use for my best boxes.

14

15

FOR THE LAST COUPLE OF CENTURIES, WHEN-ever a carpenter needed a rock-solid joint for a box, one that not only was among the sturdiest of joints but also one that helped to form square corners, more often than not the joint of choice was the box joint.

The box joint shares the attributes of a few other joints known for their high strength, most notably the dovetail joint. With its interlacing edge cuts, in fact, the box joint is really a simpler variation on dovetails. Historically, the term "dovetail" was often used interchangeably to describe true angle-cut, pin-and-tail dovetail joints as well as square-cut box joints. During the Civil War, the ordnance manuals for both the Union and Confederacy mandated that ammo boxes were to be, quoting here, "... made of white pine boards, dovetailed and nailed together." And while the arsenals did turn out ammo crates with pin-and-tail dovetails, box joints were far more common as surviving samples show.

The reason for this is simple. While both joints are very strong, each type has a particular strength. The angled surfaces of pin-and-tail dovetails meant they could be assembled in one direction only, creating a locking action that restricts movement of the joint.

14 PENCIL BOX

Items with these dovetails sometimes required little else to hold them together but the locking action, and as such these were strong, long-lasting joints. On the downside, the angled surfaces of true dovetail joints often made for very thin portions of pins and tails, affecting their strength. Also, these joints required skill and practice to cut correctly, and could often be very time-consuming.

Box joints, because the surfaces are all square cuts, can be slid together from any direction and so lack this locking action. Over time and without other means of fastening such as nails, the joints can slide apart. However, their square nature gives them two distinct benefits over true dovetails. For one thing, every part of the cut edges — usually called "fingers" as opposed to a dovetail's pins and tails — are square and the same thickness, so there are no weak spots as with a thin dovetail pin. The other is that these square joints can easily be adapted to basic machinery, a real boon in the pre-dovetail-jig 19th century. They could be made very fast, with each finger perfectly uniform. As a result, the box joint became the preferred wood joint for boxes used by industry, the military, shipping and retail. It's also why so many surviving examples are still around today, like the box I used as the basis for this project.

Among my collection of Civil War memorabilia is the domino set (seen below). I've never been able to date this antique exactly, but it's a good example of box joint use in the mid-19th century. You can also see how wood shrinkage has caused the joints to loosen; some previous owner apparently tried to reinforce the box with long-since deteriorated masking tape. But even loose, this box is still incredibly strong.

For this project, I've adjusted the dimensions of that antique box and, to make it a bit more accessible as a first attempt at box joints, enlarged the $3/16"$ joints to a more standard $1/4"$. You can make box joints by hand, of course, but in the modern shop the most common way is either on the table saw or router table. I prefer the greater control and lower risk of kickback on the router table, and so have opted for that method here using a commercially-available box joint jig. However, many people prefer the table saw for making box joints, so in a later project I'll show you how to make your own box joint jig to use on a table saw.

REFERENCE	QUANTITY	PART	STOCK	THICKNESS	(mm)	WIDTH	(mm)	LENGTH	(mm)	COMMENTS
A	2	sides	oak	1/4	(6)	2 1/4	(57)	8 1/4	(209)	
B	2	ends	oak	1/4	(6)	2 1/4	(57)	2 1/2	(64)	one will be narrower by 1/4"
C	1	sliding lid	redwood burl	1/4	(6)	2 1/4	(57)	8	(203)	
D	1	bottom	birch plywood	1/8	(3)	2 1/4	(57)	8	(203)	

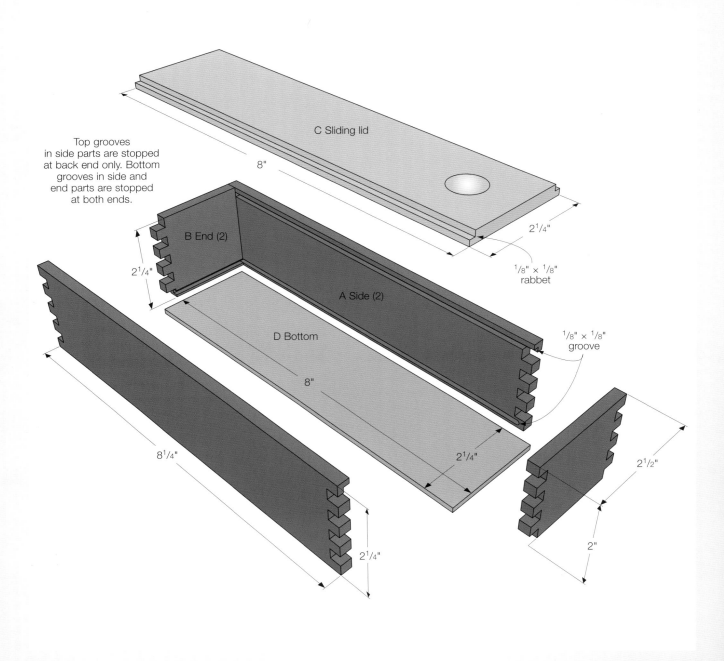

Top grooves in side parts are stopped at back end only. Bottom grooves in side and end parts are stopped at both ends.

C Sliding lid

8"

2 1/4"

1/8" × 1/8" rabbet

B End (2)

2 1/4"

A Side (2)

D Bottom

8"

2 1/4"

1/8" × 1/8" groove

8 1/4"

2 1/4"

2 1/4"

2 1/2"

2"

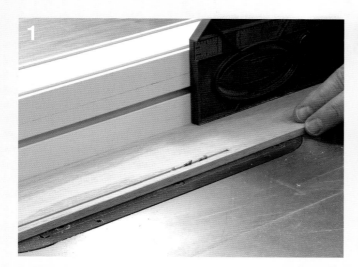

Construction

Begin by cutting your ¼" stock for the box sides and ends to width on the table saw. (Fig. 1) Before cutting your workpieces to length, give the surface that will form the inside of the box a good sanding, as in Fig. 2. It's a lot easier to do this now than after the box is assembled. Cut the sides and end workpieces to length, then arrange the pieces as shown in Fig. 3. Essentially, to achieve this arrangement just hold the four box sides upright in the shape the box will take, and let each piece flop down on the table. Now mark the pieces carefully, as you must keep them in correct orientation when cutting the joints. Mark an "A" on the sides and a "B" on the ends, and also clearly mark the top edge of each piece.

There are a couple varieties of box joint jigs, but the key to how they all work is that an index "pin" — sized to exactly match the fingers of the joint — accurately spaces each cut ensuring that they're all identical. This pin can be short and attached to the sliding fence as you'll see in a later chapter, or it can be a long pin attached to a rigid base, allowing a sliding fence to ride over it, as on the jig I'll use here and shown in Fig. 4. Despite the different pin arrangements, both work the same way.

The first step is to cut a sacrificial fence. Make a small cutout to fit over the ¼" index pin, and then attach the sacrificial fence to the jig's sliding fence. Next, set the pin the correct distance from the router bit. With this jig, the base rides in my router table's miter slot and uses expanding miter bars to lock it down. Before locking it down, move the base so the index pin is exactly ¼" away from the bit. In Fig. 5, I'm using the shank of a ¼" router bit to perfectly set the distance. With the distance set, lock the base in place.

Now, set the bit height. This is an important setting, as it controls how deeply the fingers of the joint fit together — set it too low and your fingers won't reach the surface of the joint corner, set it too high and those fingers will stick out too far. Because we're using ¼" stock, we want the bit height at ¼" so use one of your actual workpieces as a guide as in Fig. 6. When setting this height, it's best to err slightly on the high side, as it's very easy to sand slightly high box joint fingers smooth. I make it a practice of getting the bit set as perfect as I can, and then raising it a hair more.

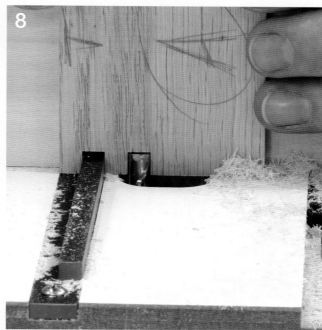

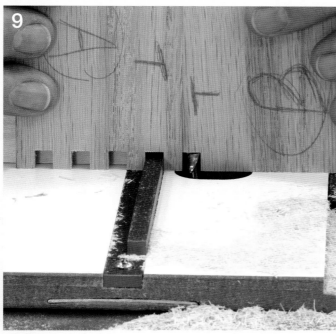

Make the first cut, starting with an "A" side piece. Hold the workpiece against the fence with the top edge butted against the index pin, and slide the fence and workpiece through the bit as in Fig. 7.

Pull the fence smoothly back, and then move the workpiece over so your first cut rests over the index pin as in Fig. 8. Now repeat the process until you've cut the fingers down the entire edge of the workpiece. Flip the workpiece end-for-end and, making sure to keep the top edge against the index pin, cut the fingers on the opposite end.

Flip the workpiece over side-for-side so the opposite face is against the fence, but the top edge is still oriented toward the center on the other side of the index pin. Place the top finger over the index pin, as in Fig. 9. This will act as a spacer that keeps the top edge of the "B" piece correctly located. Slide everything through the bit to make the first cut on the top edge of the "B" piece. Pull the fence back, and set the "A" piece aside. Move the "B" workpiece over so the first cut is against the index pin, and make the second cut as in Fig. 10, followed by the third and so on

Finger Tips

Cutting good box joints is easy, but takes a bit of practice. Here are some pointers to make the learning process go a bit faster.

• Cut the box sides a hair high. The box in this project has sides that are 2¼" high, but I cut the parts slightly larger by maybe ¹⁄₃₂". If you accidentally cut the sides too short, even a little, you'll end up with one set of fingers that's thinner than the others and you can't fix that. But to err just a bit on the larger side, and it's easy to sand the edges to the correct size.

• Set your router bit/saw blade a hair high. If your bit/blade is too low, the joint fingers won't go all the way through the stock, which is nearly impossible to fix without recutting the joints or doing a lot of sanding. Setting your cutter a hair high will make the fingers just slightly too long, which can then be quickly sanded flush.

• Use glue sparingly. Box joints literally ooze glue when sliding the fingers in place. These joints are very tight and strong and don't need a lot of glue anyway, so go easy on the stickum.

• Size boxes in increments matching the fingers. Box height is always an exact multiple of the finger size. For example, a box with ¼" joints must be in multiples of ¼". The box in this project, at 2¼" high, works fine, as would a 2" box, a 2½" box, etc. But a box 2³⁄₈" high would end up with one finger in each set of joints being mismatched at only ⅛".

until you've made all the cuts for that edge. Repeat the process for each remaining workpiece.

With all the fingers cut, dry-fit the box together to check for fit. (Fig. 11) The fit should be snug, but still slide easily together with moderate pressure.

Disassemble the dry-fit. The sliding lid needs access at the front end of the box, so cut ¼" off the top edge of this end piece. (Essentially, you're just cutting along a line from one finger to the next.)

The bottom for this box is a captured piece of ⅛" plywood, set into grooves on the inside bottom faces of the box sides before glue-up as we've already done a few times in earlier projects. We'll cut these grooves with a ⅛" straight bit on the router table. For the end pieces this groove ends at the bottom of the joints between fingers, meaning they'll be hidden inside the joints themselves when the fingers slide in. Therefore you can cut this groove straight across in a continuous pass as in Fig. 12.

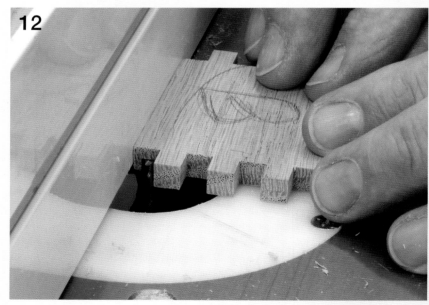

The box sides, however, have fingers on the ends where we want those grooves, so to keep the groove from being visible on the outside of the box, we'll make stopped grooves that terminate just short of the tips of the fingers. To do this, mark starting and end points on your router table's fence that will keep the groove short of the tips. Since these fingers are ¼" long, ⅛" from the ends is about as far as you want the groove to extend. Turn on your router and line up the tip of the finger with your start mark, then lower the workpiece down onto the bit as in (Fig. 13). Slide the workpiece through the bit until you reach your stop mark, and then lift the workpiece up and off the router bit. (Fig. 14)

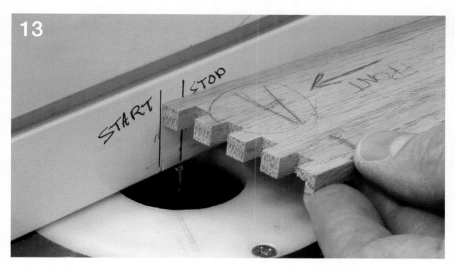

You can see the difference in the grooves in Fig. 15. On the left of the photo, you can see the stopped groove the plywood bottom slips into. The other groove is for the sliding lid. It is stopped at the rear of the box only, and continues all the way through in the front to slide the lid in. On the right of the photo is the front end piece, showing the continuous groove

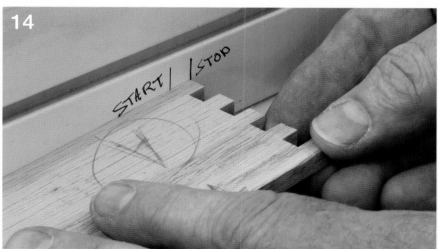

for the plywood bottom. Note in this photo how I've cut ¼" off the top of the front end piece to allow the lid to slide in.

Apply glue inside each of the fingers as in Fig. 16. You don't need a lot of glue so go sparingly; assembling finger joints creates a lot of squeeze-out, so best to minimize it beforehand. Assemble the box one side at a time, and clamp up the completed assembly till dry.

With the box done, let's move on to the lid. Cut the lid to size as noted in the cut list, and then mill a ⅛" × ⅛" rab-bet on each side (Fig. 17). Since a standard table saw blade measures ⅛", no need to set up a dado cutter. Your fence will be right up next to the blade with these cuts, so be sure to clamp on a sacrificial face.

You can cut the finger pull in a number of ways — carving chisels, router table, etc. — but I've found it very easy to do this on the drill press by chucking a bullnose router bit into it as in Fig. 18. If your drill press has a stop, it's best to engage it to control the cutting depth, and thus prevent going all the way through the lid.

You'll note in the lead photo, by the way, that I couldn't decide what kind of lid I wanted for this box, so I ended up making two: one each in redwood and walnut burl. I figure that when I give this box away I'll include both lids and let the recipient choose the lid they want to use.

What Are the Odds?

As noted in the sidebar, "Finger Tips," box height is the total of all the fingers and spaces in your box joints, where each finger and space is considered a single increment. The number of increments you use directly affects the arrangement of fingers at the corners of each joint.

An even number of increments returns the same number of fingers and spaces on each side of the joint, and there will always be an odd number of each. For example, a $2\frac{1}{2}$"-high box with $\frac{1}{4}$" joints will have five fingers and five spaces on the end of each side, as shown in Photo A. The fingers and spaces are offset on each side — each piece will have a finger at the top of one end and a space on the bottom. The mating end is just the opposite.

However, an odd number of increments returns an odd number of fingers on one end, and an even number on the mating piece. Using the $2\frac{1}{4}$"-high project box as an example, in Photo B you can see how the odd number of increments creates five fingers on one piece, and four fingers on the mating piece. Each piece has either a finger at both top and bottom, or a space at both top and bottom.

The difference between these two methods is noteworthy for two reasons. The first is aesthetic only, in that using an odd number of increments creates a box that is symmetrical — the finger arrangement is mirror-imaged on the corners left and right, top and bottom. Even-numbered increments mean that there will be a finger on one corner, and a space on the other. Whether you prefer one or the other is purely a matter of taste.

The second reason, though, is more important. To create a box with a sliding lid, as in the project box, you need symmetrical fingers at both top corners pointing toward the end of the box to accommodate a continuous groove on each side for the lid.

It's possible to cut joints on a box with an even number of increments such that you get those left/right symmetrical fingers on the top at both corners, but it requires a good bit of juggling when cutting the joints to keep everything straight. The easiest way is to simply make the height of your box an odd number of increments, and you get the symmetry automatically.

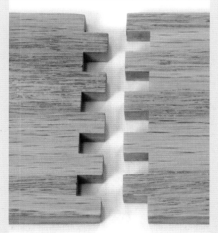

Photo A

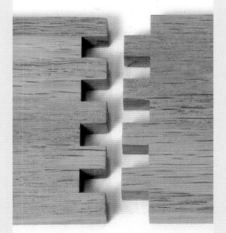

Photo B

15 KESTREL BIRD BOX

IF YOU'RE FAMILIAR WITH MY earlier F+W book *Easy To Build Birdhouses: A Natural Approach*, you know that I love birds. In fact, if you look at the countless boxes I've made over the years, I'd be willing to bet that more are bird boxes than any other kind. I make them for myself, for friends and family, I sell them from time to time, and sometimes I just make one because they're so fun to make even if I don't have a planned use for it yet.

Birds aren't real fussy when it comes to their houses, and as long as you pay strict attention to their preferred dimensions and entry-hole size, it's easy to use one basic design for a surprisingly wide variety of species. The design shown in this project, although sized for a specific bird common to my area, can be used as the basis for just about another bird you may have near you looking for a place to call home. It consists of six components, with the roof and the two sides angled at 10°, probably the most common roof angle used on bird boxes.

Behind our house is the ideal habitat for the American kestrel: a wide-open meadow that fronts the Ohio River, surrounded by trees and with a few utility poles along the highway. The kestrel — the smallest and most

common falcon in North America — coexists well with people, but they greatly appreciate nest boxes that replace the many natural tree cavities that have been eliminated by modern development.

This bird box is a mix of solid pine and plywood, which we'll give a protective coating, but feel free to use any other wood species suitable for outdoors. Western red cedar, which we'll use for the Mailbox project in a later chapter, is an especially good choice.

Construction

Cut all house components to size, angling the tops of each side 10° for the roof slope. Bevel the top edge of the house front at the same angle, as well as the rear edge of the roof.

Kestrels need a fairly large entrance hole that you can cut on the drill press with an adjustable hole cutter or hole saw. First, mark the center of the entry hole on the box front between 9" and 11" above the floor location, the distance preferred by kestrels. If using a hole cutter, first set it to 3" and chuck it into the drill press. Hole cutters and hole saws can be dangerous, so always clamp your workpiece to the drill press table as in Fig. 1, and keep your hands well clear. Note here that I'm using a piece of scrap as a backer board beneath the workpiece. When your cutter has made it through the workpiece the loose plug will come free, usually wedging in the hole cutter or hole saw. Shut off the drill press and let it spin down to a complete stop before retracting the cutter as in Fig. 2.

Before assembly, create a climbing surface on the inside of the house front by cutting shallow grooves into the wood, or by attaching wire mesh as in Fig. 3. This

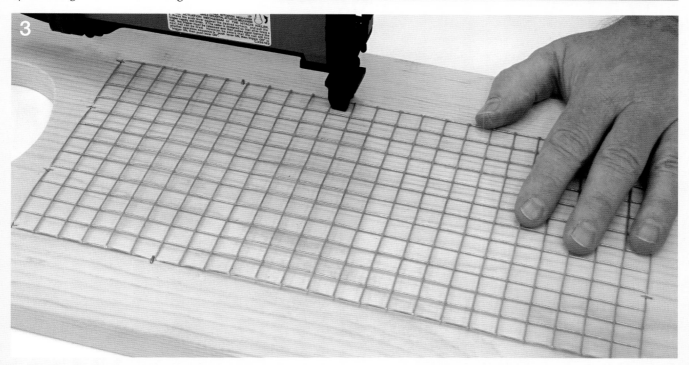

REFERENCE	QUANTITY	PART	STOCK	THICKNESS	(mm)	WIDTH	(mm)	LENGTH	(mm)	COMMENTS
A	2	sides	pine	$3/4$	(19)	9	(229)	$14^1/2$	(369)	
B	1	front	pine	$3/4$	(19)	9	(229)	16	(406)	
C	1	back	pine	$3/4$	(19)	$10^1/2$	(267)	19	(483)	
D	1	bottom	pine	$3/4$	(19)	$7^1/2$	(191)	9	(229)	
E	1	roof	plywood	$1/2$	(13)	$10^1/2$	(267)	$11^1/2$	(292)	
F	1	hinge	brass	Approx. 10" in length.						

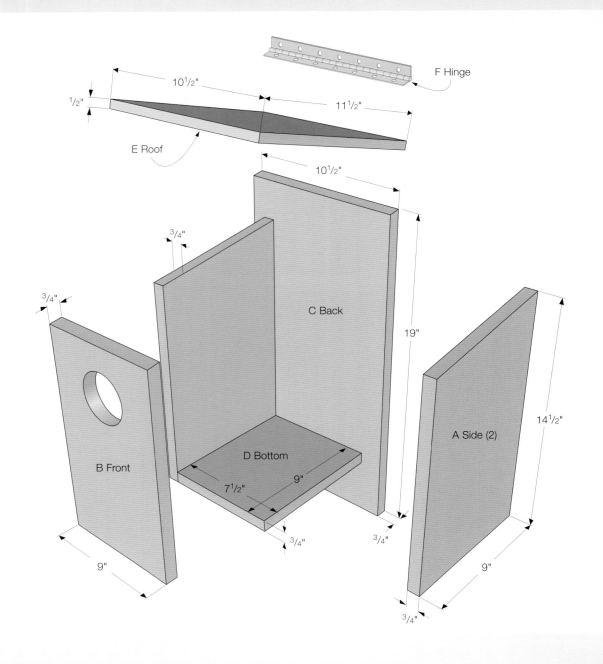

F Hinge

$10^1/2$"

$1/2$"

$11^1/2$"

E Roof

$10^1/2$"

$3/4$"

C Back

19"

$3/4$"

$14^1/2$"

B Front

A Side (2)

D Bottom

$7^1/2$"

9"

$3/4$"

$3/4$"

9"

9"

$3/4$"

will allow the nestlings to easily climb out when the time comes. Attach the front of the house to the two sides with waterproof glue and nails, (Fig. 4) followed by the floor. Center the completed box on the back, and attach with glue and nails.

You'll note here that because I plan to attach this house to a tree, the roof doesn't overhang in back as it does on a lot of bird boxes. Hold the roof in place so the beveled rear edge is against the house back, and attach the roof with a 10" continuous hinge. (A pair of smaller hinges can also be used.) The roof serves as access to the house for cleaning, but to keep it closed against the wind and potential high-climbing predators, drill countersunk pilot holes for a pair of exterior-grade screws to keep the roof firmly closed in use. (Fig. 5)

Finally, drill a few ¼" to ⅜" drainage holes into the floor of the house, and a couple ⅜" to ½" ventilation holes on each side near the back of the roof.

If you've used cedar for your kestrel box, no finish is required. But for pine and plywood you can help protect the house by painting the exterior or, as I've elected to do here, give it a good coat of deck stain as in Fig. 6. Always keep in mind that when adding a coating of any kind to a birdhouse, use it on exterior surfaces only — don't get any paint or stain on the inside of the house, or on the inner edge of the entry hole.

Mount the house on a tree at least 10' above the ground (although 15'-30' high is better), preferably at the edge of a wide, flat clearing or meadow. The perfect location will include other high perches scattered around the meadow, such as other tall trees or utility poles, as kestrels like to perch high over a flat area as they scan for prey. Kestrels don't actually build nests, so it's a good idea to

put a few inches of wood shavings or chips (not sawdust, which is too fine), or a mix of dry leaves and small twigs in the house before mounting.

Variations for Other Bird Boxes

As noted earlier, this exact same box design is perfect for other birds as long as you keep some things in mind.

• Cater to the bird: Your first step in designing a bird box is to find out what preferences your intended resident has, and adjust this basic bird box plan accordingly. There are four key elements you'll need to alter to suit a particular bird — the interior dimensions, size of the entry hole, overall box height and the height of the entrance hole over the box floor. Just about any good reference on birds will include a chart of these preferences organized by species. While not an aspect of the box design itself, a final consideration to keep in mind is how high and where you'll want to mount your box. This will vary from one species to the next.

• Include a means of access: You'll want to clean the house out from time to time, so include a means of opening the box. For the kestrel house, because you need to supply nesting material as well as clean it out occasionally, I've fitted it with a hinged lid. Alternatively, you can install a hinged floor. A method I use a lot for bird boxes of this design is to make one entire side of the box in a lift-up manner as shown in Fig. 7. This is easy to do by driving pivot nails on both edges of one side near the top. The bottom can be secured with screws, or a twist latch

• Ventilation is a must: Bird boxes can become incredibly hot inside, especially when mounted in the sun. We've provided that in this box by simply drilling ventilation holes near the top on each side, but you can see two other methods in Fig. 8. Any corner near the top of the box can be notched before assembly as in the finch box shown on the left in this photo. If you opt to make access by means of a tilting side as in the bluebird box on the right in the photo, just make that side about ¼" shorter on that side. Note the twist latch here that keeps the lift-up side closed.

7

• Provide drainage: There's no way to prevent rain from entering a bird box through the entry, so you must give it somewhere to go. The boxes in Fig. 9. show a couple of methods. On the left in the photo I've notched each of the four corners of the box bottom before installing it. On the right simple drilled holes — as we did for the kestrel box — do the trick. Box drainage not only lets water out, but air in to do double duty in keeping nestlings dry. As warm air rises and exits the box through the entry hole and ventilation at the top of the box, cooler dry air rises up through the nest, helping to keep it dry.

SO FAR, WE'VE DONE A COUPLE PROJECTS using very thin stock. And, so far, it's assumed you purchased it from a specialty woodworking supplier. With this project — a holder for business cards — let's take a look at making thin stock yourself. Although the cutterheads of most thickness planers can be lowered to within ⅛" of the planer table, this measurement isn't always exact. It's also not particularly easy to feed stock that thin through a planer, and depending on your planer there may even be a danger of running the cutterhead all the way down into

the table and risking damage to the cutter blades at a minimum, and possibly the cutterhead itself. So is it back to ordering from a supplier? Well, sure, there's always that option, but let's start this project, made with nothing thicker than ¼", by making our own thin stock. Here's a safe, easy way.

First, to do this you'll need some double-stick tape. Woodworking suppliers sell this, and it's used a lot for woodturning to attach blanks to faceplates. In a pinch, you could also use carpet tape if you already happen to have some.

16 BUSINESS CARD HOLDER

You'll also need a sled board. This can be anything you have around the shop that's wider and longer than the stock you'll be planing. Make sure your sled board itself is milled to a uniform thickness. I accomplished this by giving a piece of 1"-thick walnut a few passes through the planer to create a smooth, flat surface. Now, stick your working stock to the top of the sled board with the double-stick tape. Don't use full strips of the tape, and certainly don't use it over the entire width and length of your workpiece — you may never get it off. Instead, tear off shorter pieces of the tape and apply them at key points around the front and side edges, plus a few down the center. Press down to ensure that's it's stuck securely. Since this project calls for ⅛" stock, I started by securing a piece of ¼" bird's-eye maple to my sled board.

Construction

Set your planer to the combined thickness of the piggyback workpieces, which keeps the cutterhead well away from the table and allows for easier stock feed. Begin running the joined workpieces through your planer as in Fig. 1. Each time you run this through, recheck your workpiece to be sure it's still securely attached, and continue planing until the workpiece is at the target thickness.

With the desired thickness reached, peel the thin stock from the top of the sled board. You may need to use a putty knife or other thin tool to get underneath one corner or edge. With the thin stock freed of the sled board, remove any remaining tape. If there's any adhesive on the thin workpiece, remove it with mineral spirits.

Cut the two face pieces from your freshly milled ⅛" stock. Select one piece to be the front — you'll probably want to use the piece with the best figure — and drill a 1" hole through the center as in Fig. 2. This hole serves a dual purpose: It acts as a window to see that the box is filled with cards, and should the cards become jammed inside after inadvertently pushing too many cards in you can use your thumb to slide them out the top. Create a slight bevel around what will be the outer edge of the opening with a piece of rolled sandpaper (Fig. 3).

REFERENCE	QUANTITY	PART	STOCK	THICKNESS	(mm)	WIDTH	(mm)	LENGTH	(mm)	COMMENTS
A	2	front/back faces	bird's eye maple	1/8	(3)	2⁵⁄₈	(67)	4¹⁄₂	(115)	
B	2	long edge spacers	maple	1/4	(6)	1/4	(6)	4	(102)	
C	1	bottom edge spacer	maple	1/4	(6)	1/4	(6)	2¹⁄₈	(54)	
D	1	flip lid	maple	1/4	(6)	1/2	(13)	2¹¹⁄₁₆	(68)	
E	1	lid pivot	birch dowel	3/32	(2.5)	1/2	(13)			

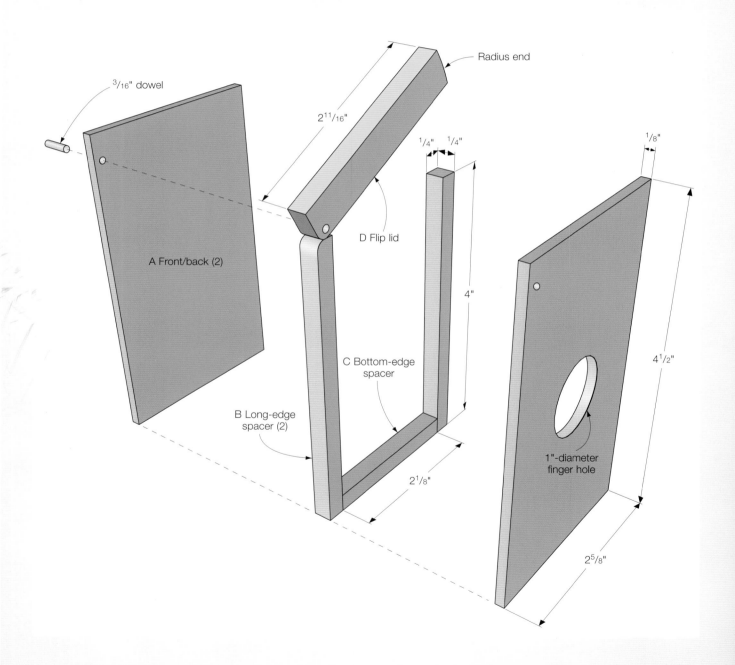

3/16" dowel

Radius end

2¹¹⁄₁₆"

1/4" 1/4"

1/8"

A Front/back (2)

D Flip lid

4"

4¹⁄₂"

C Bottom-edge
spacer

B Long-edge
spacer (2)

1"-diameter
finger hole

2¹⁄₈"

2⁵⁄₈"

Cut the box edge spacers and flip-top lid from ¼" maple. (If you prefer, you can make the spacers from a contrasting wood species, such as walnut or cherry.) Mark the bottom-rear corner of the flip lid with a curve as in Fig. 4. This curve will allow the lid to pivot freely without the back corner of the lid hitting the top of the rear spacer. You'll note in this photo that I've also rounded the top of that rear spacer — there's no mechanical need for this as the pivoting allowance only needs to be made on the flip-top lid itself, but I felt the back-to-back curves on the rear of the card box pre-

sented a nicer appearance, as we'll look at more closely a bit later. With the curve marked, form the curved shape with a disk sander or sanding block.

Glue and clamp the spacers in place on the bottom and side edges of the inside of the front face, as in Fig. 5. To help keep the pieces straight, I've marked each gluing face with an "X."

As you probably noticed in the Spool Box project, I very much like to put a finish on the inaccessible spaces inside boxes even if I have to apply it before the project is

assembled. So, before gluing the back in place I've rubbed a linseed oil finish on the inside surfaces. In Fig. 6, you can see how I've attached a bit of masking tape around the edges of the back piece to keep the oil finish off, thus ensuring a good gluing surface. Allow the finish to dry, and give it a good rubbing out. Then remove the tape, and glue and clamp the back in place. Allow the assembly to dry thoroughly, and then sand all edges flush and smooth.

Gluing the pivot dowel in place is slightly tricky because of the size of the workpieces involved, but straightforward. Slightly round over the front of the flip lid — you want this to be a good "thumbable" surface as you can see in the finished photos — then slip the lid into place. Drill a 3/32" hole trough the box and lower back corner of the lid, as in Fig. 7. This hole should be centered 1/8" from the curved pivoting corner. To help serve as a guide, you can see how I've marked the locations of the edge spacers on the face in pencil.

Now comes the trickiest part, gluing in the pivot dowel without getting glue into the internal portions of the flip lid. On a secure, flat surface, slip a longer portion of dowel into the drilled face hole and through the flip lid. Push the dowel in until it's all the way through the first face and the flip lid, but not into the face on the other side. Keep a

close eye on the hole in the back face, and stop pushing the dowel through when it just touches the edge of that hole before actually entering it. Place a drop of glue into the hole on the back face, then lay the assembly on your flat surface. Spread a bit of glue around the portion of the dowel that will slide into the hole on the top face as in Fig. 8. You don't need a lot of glue in either of these two locations, so go sparingly. Now, tap the dowel down the rest of the way through the assembly till it bottoms out on your work surface, but no further. Bingo! That pivot dowel now has glue securing it only to the faces, with none on the inside of the assembly.

Trim the extra dowel and wipe off any excess glue squeeze-out (you'll have some on both sides). When dry, sand the pivot dowel flush on both faces, followed by a good overall sanding with increasingly finer grits of sandpaper. Again, because of the small size of all the workpieces in this project, it's best to stay away from the machines and hand-sand only. With all sanding dust removed, I gave my business card box several coats of boiled linseed oil, and rubbed everything out to a soft satin sheen.

I promised earlier that we'd take a closer look at some of the details when the box was completed, and in Fig. 8 you can get a close look at the pivot point on the back. You can see how those two curved edge spacers not only allow the lid to pivot unimpeded, but complement the lines on the back far better than just one curved corner on the lid and a straight corner on the spacer below it would have.

As to the pivot action itself, to open the box just flip the rounded tip of the lid (Fig. 9) up with the tip of your thumb. This is a good time to discuss variations. Because I'm right-handed, I've oriented to flip part of the lid to allow the face of the business card holder to appear "up" when opening. If you or the intended recipient of your holder is a lefty, consider reorienting the pivot point to the opposite top corner of the box.

For other variations, you can obviously use just about any wood species you like, but it's best to stick to hardwood — you'll need the strength of hardwood for these small workpieces. I liked the look of square corners on my card box, but you could round each corner if you prefer. This box, with its ¼"-thick edge spacers, accommodates 30 business cards made with regular laser-printer business card stock. However, the thickness of professionally produced cards varies a lot — and is almost always thicker than printer card stock — so a box of the same size will hold fewer cards. I wanted a slim profile here, but you could easily increase the thickness of the edge spacers a bit to allow the completed card box to hold more cards than this example.

8

9

17 MAILBOX

WHAT'S MY FAVORITE TIME OF the day? Why, shop time, of course. But my second favorite has to be when I hear the loud muffler on my mailman's truck, because that means it's mail time. Yeah, I'm a mail junkie, and I await the sound of the mailbox flap being opened each day with more anticipation than a family dog does when looking for an excuse to bark. With that in mind, it probably isn't surprising to find a mailbox project among this collection.

This particular design is a simple one made in a great outdoor wood, Western red cedar. Cedar is a perfect choice for any project intended for outdoor use, as it's resistant to both the weather and insects. After a bit of exposure it fades to an attractive silver patina. It works easily with both hand and power tools. And you won't find a wood that fills the shop with a better aroma when you're working it than cedar.

While a true pleasure to work with, you have to keep a couple things in mind about cedar. First, it can split easily so always drill pilot holes before driving screws. Also, cedar is almost always milled in such a way

that one side is smooth, while the other side has a lovely rough texture. Unless you opt to sand out that roughness so both sides match, lay out components carefully so you orient those surfaces in the same direction — either rough-out or smooth-out — for a consistent appearance.

Finally, and most importantly, although cedar is sold nominally as being ¾" it's frequently a bit thicker, usually ranging from ¾" to ⅞". In fact, pick up two pieces and they're not likely to be the same. Because all the dimensions in this project assume a thickness of ¾", be prepared to make slight adjustments to various components to take into account the true thickness of the stock you're using. The difference may not seem like much, but that extra ⅛" over a regular ¾" board can compound quickly in projects with multiple pieces. In a box, for example, that extra ⅛" on each side makes the box ¼" larger. Add more components, and the variance can be even greater. With that in mind, always try to take components for a project from the same board, and always measure to verify the exact thickness.

Construction

Begin by laying out all the components. Note in Fig. 1 that I'm using a single board — I'll have consistent thickness for all the parts — and also dodging defects like knots as I go. You can make your mailbox with either the smooth or rough side facing out, but I've opted for rough-out and am sketching out the components accordingly.

I've noted earlier in the book that when I cut parts in pairs I try to double them up when possible, ensuring perfectly matched pieces. Since the parts layout had to take knots into consideration, there was a bit of waste around most of the parts, making it easy to do larger rough cuts first, then attach the two components together with a few brads before cutting them out on the band saw. (Fig. 2) I found it easiest to do the angled cuts on the band saw first, and then make the last 90° cut on the table saw as in Fig. 3.

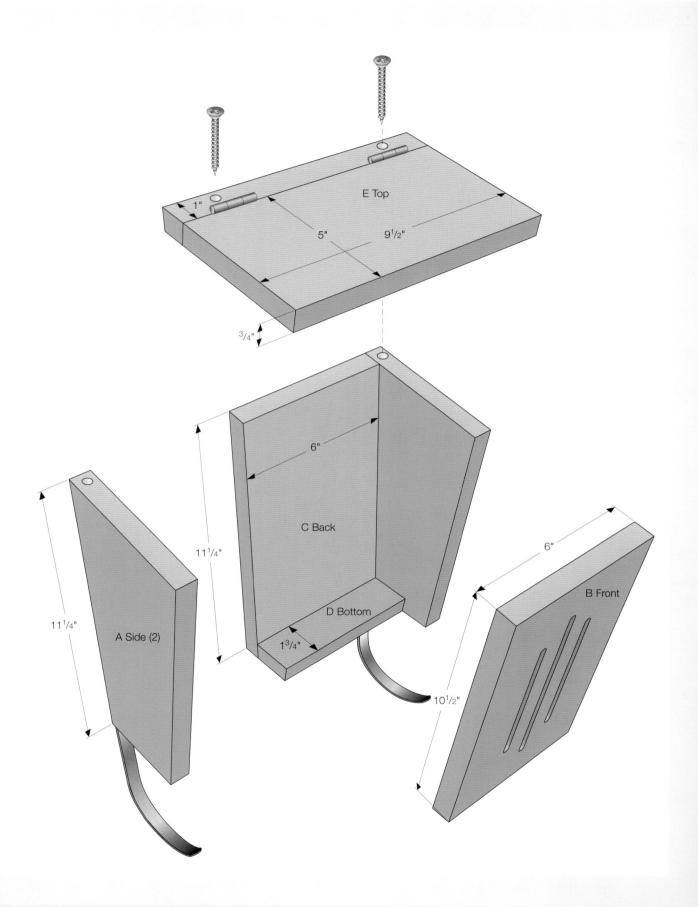

E Top

1"

5"

9 1/2"

3/4"

6"

C Back

11 1/4"

A Side (2)

11 1/4"

D Bottom

1 3/4"

B Front

6"

10 1/2"

REFERENCE	QUANTITY	PART	STOCK	THICKNESS	(mm)	WIDTH	(mm)	LENGTH	(mm)	COMMENTS
A	2	sides	western red cedar	³⁄₄	(19)	5¹⁄₂	(140)	11¹⁄₄	(285)	
B	1	front	western red cedar	³⁄₄	(19)	6	(152)	10⁵⁄₈	(270)	
C	1	back	western red cedar	³⁄₄	(19)	6	(152)	11¹⁄₄	(285)	
D	1	bottom	western red cedar	³⁄₄	(19)	1³⁄₄	(44)	6	(152)	
E	1	top	western red cedar	³⁄₄	(19)	9¹⁄₂	(242)	6¹⁄₂	(165)	Size before cut in two.

Cedar is nominal ³⁄₄", but actual thickness of cedar often varies. Measure stock and alter dimensions accordingly.

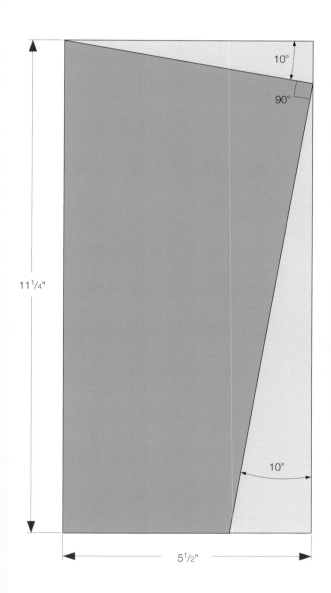

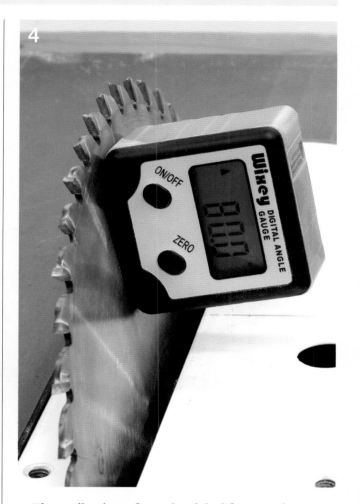

The mailbox leans forward and the lift-up top slopes at 10° angles, so you'll need to bevel a few edges. Set the blade on your table saw to 80°. (Fig. 4) I never trust the saw's built-in angle indicator, but a digital gauge gives me a perfect setting. With the saw set, bevel the top edge of the box back (Part C) so it angles down toward the front; the front edge of the box floor (Part D) so it angles up; the bottom edge of the box front (Part B) angling toward the back;

and the rear edge of the box top (Part E) angling toward the back. If you make the cuts in this order, the box top will be the last beveled cut you need to make. (Fig. 5)

Right after making that cut, return the saw blade to 90° and slice a 1½" piece off the rear section of the box top as in Fig. 6. This thinner piece will be anchored to the mailbox, with hinges attaching the front portion to it to create the lift-up lid.

I wanted a means to be able to tell at a glance if there was mail in the box, and decided that three narrow slots would not only accomplish this, but would lend a nice detail to the front. We made some stopped cuts on the router table for earlier projects and these are done the same way,

but this time you'll make multiple cuts of varying lengths in the same workpiece.

You'll want to cut these slots through the front face to keep any possible tear-out hidden inside the box, so layout the three slots on the inside face of the box in pencil, centering a 5"-long slot in the middle. Now, add two 3"-long slots 1" to either side of the middle one, centered top to bottom. Draw perpendicular lines from the ends of these slots to the edge of the workpiece, and then use the lines to mark your router table fence for stop and start locations. Once you've set your fence the correct distance (2" for the outer slots, and 3" for the middle one), you're ready to rout.

Turn on the router and align the workpiece with your start mark, then carefully lower the workpiece onto the bit. Slide the workpiece smoothly until the trailing end of the workpiece reaches the stop mark on the fence. Now, carefully lift the trailing end of the workpiece up and off the bit. Repeat the procedure for the other two slots. You can see this three-part sequence in Figs. 7-9.

Most of the glue joints on this box are edge-to-face joints that are

plenty strong with no need of mechanical reinforcement; however, you will want to add a bit of reinforcement to the two butt joints. The first of these is the box floor. You could probably skip these since the floor is "captured" inside very strong edge/face joints, but a couple brads through the back will not only guarantee extra strength for the box floor, but will also make assembly a bit easier. Apply waterproof glue to the rear edge of the floor and attach it ¼" up from the inside-bottom edge of the box back, then secure it with three brads through the back while the glue dries as in Fig. 10.

Now we'll assembly the box by moving around the four sides. Apply glue to the back edge of one of the sides (Fig. 11) and one edge of the floor and clamp the side in place. When the glue dries, apply glue to the mating edge of the front and the front edge of the floor, and locate the front ¼" back from the front edge of the box; it should nestle firmly against the front edge of the floor (Fig. 12). When the assembly is dry, put glue on the remaining exposed box edges and the last end of the floor, and clamp the final side in place (Fig. 13).

The rough-out appearance of the cedar looks great, but all the cut edges are per-

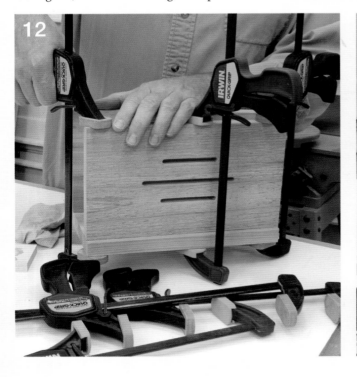

fectly smooth. If you want them to match the rough texture of the box, here's a trick. Drag a wire wheel — the kind used in drills to remove rust — along each edge to rough it up as in Fig. 14. Wear gloves when you do this as the wires on these things are quite sharp, and go sparingly: a little roughing up goes a long way.

With the main box done, let's move on to the lift-up lid. We need to cut a pair of mortises in each of the two pieces that make up the top (Part E), and it'll be easier and more accurate to do these at the same time. Clamp these two pieces together so the mating ends are aligned, and layout your hinges about 1" in from each side, as in Fig. 15. Demarcate the ends of the mor-

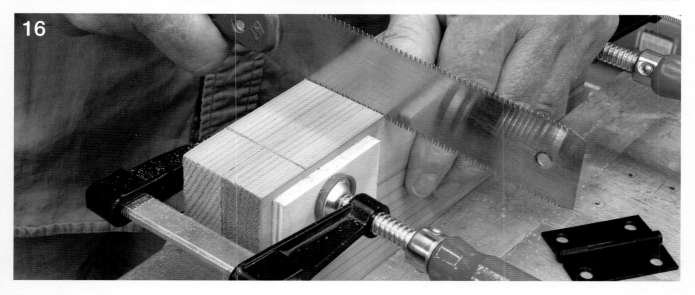

tises with a knife, chisel or a fine-cut saw as I'm doing in Fig. 16.

Use a chisel to pare out the mortises. (Fig. 17) Be sure to stop frequently and use one of the hinges to check the depth as you go. When you're satisfied with your work, drill pilot holes and screw the hinges in place. As you can see in Fig. 18, the good-looking black hinges I bought didn't come with matching screws so I used some weatherproof 1" screws I had on hand. When the project is complete, I'll dab a bit of black paint over the heads so they don't look so out-of-place.

Before attaching the lid, cut shallow mortises for the magazine holders. You can find these at just about any home center. (As an alternative, you can make your own from flat bar stock and paint them, purchase a cheap plastic mailbox that includes a pair, or skip them.) The width, depth and length of these mortises depends on holders you find. Mine were ½" wide, so that's the size bit I used, making the mortise deep enough to accommodate the thickness of the holders as well as the screw heads so everything is recessed beneath the back

134

20

21

surface. Although open on the bottom of the box, this is a stopped mortise created the same way as the slots we cut into the front earlier. (Fig. 19) We'll need to rest the box flat on a work surface to attach the top, so don't install the holders yet.

Because the lid assembly is attached by means of a butt joint, screws are definitely needed to mount it. Drill pilot holes first, then apply a bit of waterproof glue on the top edge of the box back before driving your screws home, as in Fig. 20.

Lay the mailbox down on its face — you'll need to open the lid a bit to do this — and screw the two magazine holders in place. (Fig. 21) How you mount or hang your new mailbox will depend on where you plan to locate it, and the composition of the mounting surface. If you plan to screw it in place against a wall, drill mounting holes through the back of the box making sure they're in-line with the routed slots on the front. This will allow you to slip a screwdriver through the slots to tighten the screws. You could also attach hangers to the back for mounting.

With the mailbox securely in place, the last step, of course, is to wait for the mailman to arrive.

MY WIFE AND I — OUR WHOLE FAMILY, REALLY — love to play games. Board games, tile games, dice games, card games, you name it. Among our favorites are card games that use a special deck such as Phase 10, Uno, Skip-Bo and Five Crowns. We play these so much that it doesn't take long for the flimsy cardboard box the cards came in to fall apart. These games also use very large decks (Phase 10 and Uno each have 108 cards, while Five Crowns has 116 and Skip-Bo a whopping 162), and keeping all these cards corralled during play is sometimes problematic.

This project, which is really two nesting boxes, solves both problems. The card tray box has two compartments that hold the draw pile and the discard pile. Cutouts on the sides or ends make the cards easier to take out. The main box holds the card tray box when not in use, and has a bit of extra room over the tray to hold a note pad for scoring.

At first glance at the length of the text and all the photos you might think this is a difficult project, but it's really not. True, there are a lot of steps; however, keep in mind that we're really making not one, but two boxes here at the same time. You can make these in any order, but I've begun with the main box.

In the Business Card Holder project, I addressed the issue of creating your own stock for a project. We'll revisit that with this project, but with another process — resawing. I've made a number of these boxes, but

18 GAME BOX

the first one I made was for my parents, who were living in the Allegheny National Forest in Pennsylvania at the time. During a visit there I helped my dad clear a downed cherry tree, and we cut up some nice, big chunks that I crammed in the car to take home. (I had so much wood shoved in there, the back end almost dragged.) To make that first game box a bit more special for them, I made it from some of that cherry.

More than a decade later, I still have a few chunks of that cherry squirreled — now very well seasoned — so I thought it was time to pull some out for this project. We'll resaw one of those chunks to make the ⅜" stock we'll need. Milling stock that you've cut from the tree yourself is very rewarding, plus it carries with it another benefit for the box maker: By using resawn stock, you can make a box where all four corners have continuous grain.

I've mentioned continuous grain in some of the earlier projects like Kim's Christmas Box, noting that box sides cut from the same board will have three corners with continuous grain; all you have to do is be sure to keep the pieces adjacent to each other in the same order in which you cut them, and the grain will appear to flow around the box on three corners. You're out of luck on that fourth corner, though, since those points always come from opposite ends of the board, so it's best to keep that corner in the back of the box where it's less noticeable. With resawing, however, when you cut two pieces of stock from a thicker board, the touching faces — the faces created by the cut — have mirrored grain. Cut your box sides in the correct order, which I'll show you shortly, and you'll get a perfect flow on all four sides.

Construction

First, though, let's get resawing. Start by jointing a smooth face on the top and bottom of your slab; the jointed bottom makes feeding through the band saw steadier, while the smooth top side allows your cut lines to be clearly seen. Also, once the individual boards are resawn free of the slab, you'll already have straight edges to ride your table saw's fence.

Mark your slab for cutting. Since I needed a quantity of ⅜" stock for this project, I marked the slab for ½" cuts — that extra ⅛" gives me some working room for cleaning up the cut faces. Work your way through the slab one board at a time, as in Fig. 1. Note in this photo that after starting the cut, I've slipped a sliver of wood into the kerf to prevent it from closing up and pinching the blade, which sometimes happens when resawing.

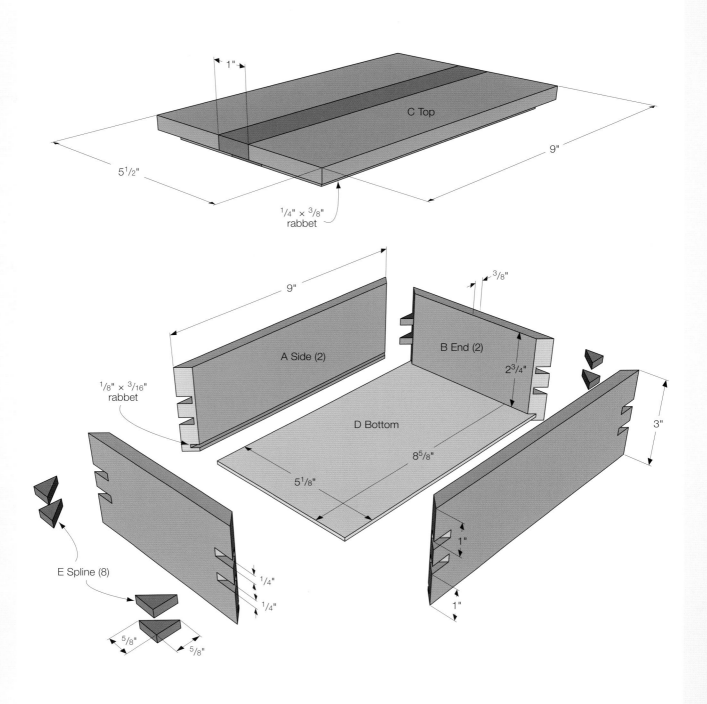

C Top

1"

5¹/₂"

9"

$^1/_4"$ × $^3/_8"$
rabbet

9"

$^3/_8"$

A Side (2)

B End (2)

$^1/_8"$ × $^3/_{16}"$
rabbet

2³/₄"

3"

D Bottom

8⁵/₈"

5¹/₈"

1"

E Spline (8)

$^1/_4"$

$^1/_4"$

1"

$^5/_8"$

$^5/_8"$

GAME BOX • INCHES (MILLIMETERS)

REFERENCE	QUANTITY	PART	STOCK	THICKNESS	(mm)	WIDTH	(mm)	LENGTH	(mm)	COMMENTS
Main Box										
A	2	sides	cherry	$3/8$	(10)	3	(76)	9	(229)	
B	2	ends	cherry	$3/8$	(10)	3	(76))	$5^1/2$	(140)	
C	1	lid	cherry/walnut	$5/8$	(16)	$5^1/2$	(140)	9	(229)	Dimension is finished size of lid.
D	1	bottom	birch plywood	$1/8$	(3)	$5^1/8$	(130)	$8^5/8$	(219)	
E	8	splines	walnut	$1/4$	(6)	1	(25)	1	(25)	
Card Box										
F	2	sides	cherry	$1/4$	(6)	$1^3/4$	(45)	7	(178)	
G	2	ends	mahogany	1	(25)	$1^3/4$	(45)	$4^1/2$	(115)	
H	1	bottom	cherry	$1/4$	(6)	$4^1/4$	(108)	7	(178)	
J	1	divider	cherry	$1/4$	(6)	$1^1/2$	(38)	$4^1/4$	(108)	

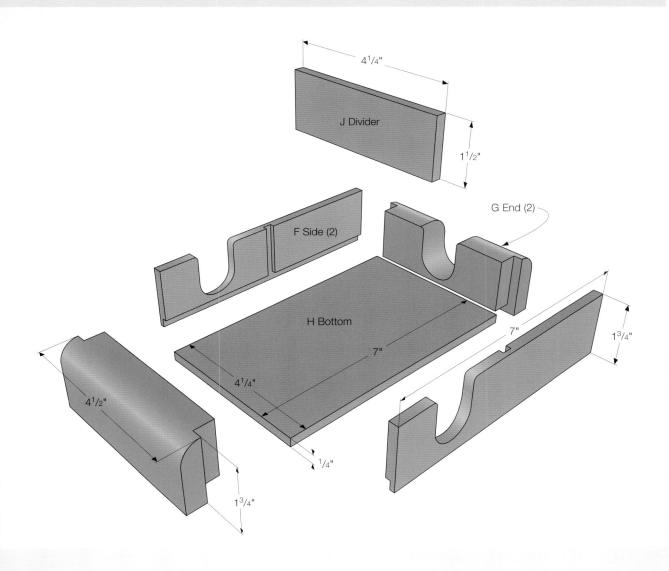

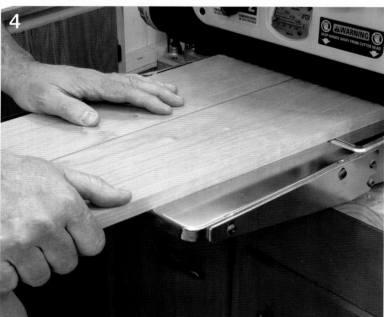

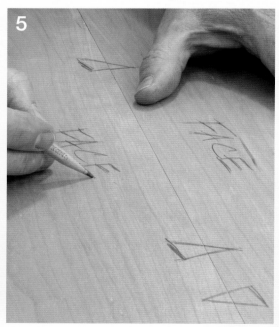

Mark the ends of your resawn stack so you can keep the board orientation straight after cleaning up the faces and milling them to final thickness. (Fig. 2) Clean up one face on the jointer, as I'm doing in Fig. 3, but don't go overboard; stop as soon as you've got the face perfectly smooth. Now move to the planer to bring the boards to thickness and clean up the opposite faces. (Fig. 4)

Using the end marks you made earlier, put your two boards into the same orientation they where in when you cut them, then just allow the two boards to flop open like a book in a process called book-matching, which we used on the spalted maple lid insert for Kim's Christmas Box. You can see in Fig. 5 how the grain is mirror imaged. These two faces will become the outside of the box, so to keep them straight, add witness marks to help you positively identify the orientation. You'll need these face marks, as we're about to cut off the ones you made on the ends. With your witness marks in place, rip the two boards to the 3" width as indicated on the cut list.

To make the grain on all four corners continuous, we'll cut one side "A" and one end "B" from one board, and the other side "A" and end "B" from the other. Each board, then, should first be cut to 14⅝" in length (the combined length of a 9" side and a 5½" end, plus ⅛" for the saw blade's kerf between the two) on the table saw as in Fig. 6. Now, cut a side and an end from each board, and line them up end-to-end A-B-A-B with the continuous faces up, and you'll see that the grain flows smoothly from one piece to the next. Marks these clearly A-B-A-B, and remember that these faces (which were in the center of the slab before you cut) will now become the outside faces of the box. (Fig. 7) To keep the A-B order straight, you might also want to number the sides 1 through 4.

Cut a ⅛" groove for the plywood bottom 3/16" deep on the bottom-inside edge of all the side and end pieces, placing the groove ⅛" from the bottom edge. (Fig. 8) This would also be a good time to cut the plywood bottom to the dimensions shown in the cut list.

Set your table saw to 45° and cut corner miters on the ends of each piece as in Fig. 9. Take your time, and cut off only enough to make the miters.

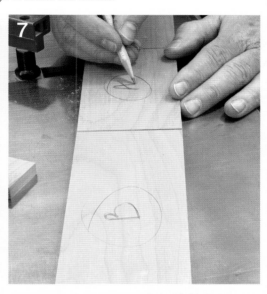

We'll assemble the box the same way we've done the other miter-corner boxes in earlier projects by applying packing tape to the outside corners, then laying the four connected pieces inside-up to apply the glue. (Fig. 10) In this photo, you can easily see the continuous grain running through the miter joints. Now, insert the plywood bottom into one of the grooves, and just fold the box up around the bottom as in Fig. 11. You can use more packing tape to keep the box closed, or use a set of band clamps as I'm doing in Fig. 12. I prefer band clamps when making mitered boxes, as there's no danger of one of the pieces of tape letting loose. With the box clamped up, remove any glue squeeze-out with a damp rag, and allow the clamped assembly to dry.

Meanwhile, let's move on to the lid. I've made the lid out of the same cherry used for the box, but I've added a walnut accent strip down the lid that will match the corner splines we'll add to the box later. Make the lid by gluing a 1" strip of walnut between two pieces of cherry, and clamp up till dry (Fig. 13). If you're wondering why

I used such a long piece of walnut, there's a good reason. After the glued-up lid is dry, I'll need to run it through the planer to bring it to uniform thickness, but unfortunately the two pieces of cherry I had on hand were too short for planing. (The minimum length for workpieces on most benchtop planers is 12".) Using that extra-long walnut strip increases the effective planing length of the lid so that it runs through the planer with no problem. This is a good trick to keep in mind when planing any too-short stock.

With the lid milled to its 5/8" thickness, trim it to size on the table saw. (Fig. 14) With the lid cut to size, mill a 3/8" rabbet 1/4" deep around the underside of the lid. In Fig. 15, I'm using my router table fitted with a straight bit, but you could also cut this rabbet with a dado set installed in your table saw.

Now, if you noticed that the grain of the top during the glue-up in Fig. 13 is way different from the grain of the finished lid in the lead photo for this chapter, then you've got a keen eye indeed. You can see the reason for this in Fig. 16. There was a really tight knot and small void right in the edge of that first lid that was completely invisible before routing. When the router cut into it, it knocked an ugly chunk out of my lid, turning it into scrap. Oh, well, it happens sometimes. However, when I glued-up a second lid, a crack appeared on one end when I cut it to size, as you can see in the same photo. I easily repaired the crack with some cyanoacrylate glue ("super" glue), but couldn't trim the lid any more to remove the staining caused by the glue without making the lid too small. Strike two. Fortunately, third time was the charm and yielded the lid you see in the finished photo. In the meantime, I'll hang on to those two failed lids and adapt them to smaller boxes in some future project.

With the lid done, let's move back to the main box to create the splined corners. As I noted in the first chapter, miter joints are usually plenty strong for boxes since they don't see a lot of stresses on the joints. Still, a bit of extra strength is never a bad thing, and I really like the way splines accent a box.

You can cut the slots for corner splines on either the table saw or router table, but with either method you'll need to create a very simple jig like the one in Fig. 17. There really isn't much to the jig, and it goes together quickly. First, make a 45° crosscut in a short length of 2×4. Flip one of the pieces over to create a "cradle," which will hold the 90° corner of your box, and attach the two pieces tip-to-tip to a piece of 1×4 stock with screws driven through the back. Be

absolutely certain that the screws are driven above where the cutter will go by putting them at least 2" above the cutting edge.

Determine where you want your splines to be — for this box, I located them at 1" from the top and bottom edges of the box — and set the fence on your saw or router table accordingly. Set the height of your dado set or router bit carefully, as you don't want to cut all the way into the inside of the box. For this box, a height of no more than $7/16$" works well. Run the jig one time through the cutter to create a channel, which will allow you to run the jig smoothly through the real cuts later. As a plus, the bulk of the jig acts as a backer to prevent tear-out in the box corners when cutting the slots.

Set the box in the jig, turn on the saw or router, and run everything through as in Fig. 18. Cut four spline slots with the box oriented with the box opening facing away from the fence, then flip the box with the open side in and make four more slots.

Cut eight small splines from $1/4$" walnut and glue them into the slots on all four corners. (Figs. 19 & 20), When the splines have dried, trim them any way you like — I'm using the band saw in Fig. 21 — and then sand the splines flush and smooth with the surface.

That's it for the main box. Give everything a good sanding with increasing grits of sandpaper, and apply the finish of your choice. For this box I've chosen a wiping varnish, but a rubbed-out oil finish would also look great. When the finishing is complete, line the bottom of the box with felt in the color of your choice.

The Card Box

Now, let's move on to part two of this box project which is, well, another box project. This one holds the cards and is sized to fit inside the main box. For this one, I've elected to use the same cherry as in the main box, but instead of walnut for the accent wood I've opted for mahogany. The components of this box are on the small side, so I'll show you a trick for making them that's safer and easier by doing most of the work before cutting out the individual parts.

Start with the ends (Part G) by cutting a piece of 1" mahogany to 4½" wide, measured in the direction of the grain. The length of this workpiece, measured against the grain, isn't critical as long as it's more than 3½", the combined 1¾" height of both end pieces. My workpiece, for example, was about 5½" long, which makes for a workpiece large enough to make the routing we'll need to do a lot easier.

Cut a ½"-wide rabbet ¼" deep on all four sides of this workpiece. That's a pretty high rabbet, so in Fig. 22 you can see that I'm sneaking up on the final dimension by making a couple of passes, raising the bit between cuts to achieve the full cut. I've used a straight bit in my router table to make these rabbets, but you can use a dado set in a table saw.

Once you've milled the rabbets, cut a 1¾" slice off each end to create both end pieces, as in Fig. 23. It's as simple as that. Instead of attempting to cut fairly large rabbets on such small pieces — an uncomfortable procedure at best — you've cut them on a larger workpiece and cut the finished pieces from it.

Create the two sides for the card box the same way by cutting a piece of ¼" cherry 7" wide, again measured with the grain. The length of this piece should be at least double the 1¾" height of the sides. Now mill a ¼" wide rabbet ⅛" deep into the exact center of this workpiece for the card box divider. You can see in Fig. 24 that I'm using a backer board (yeah, it's

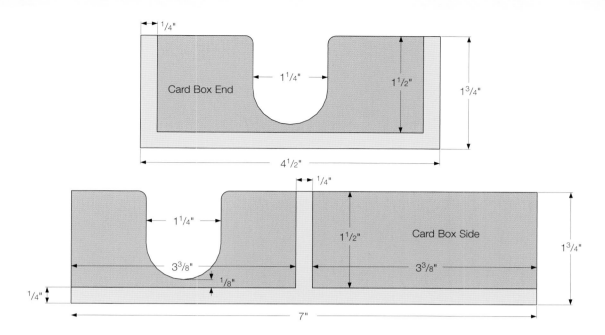

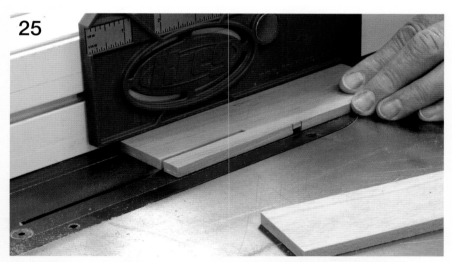

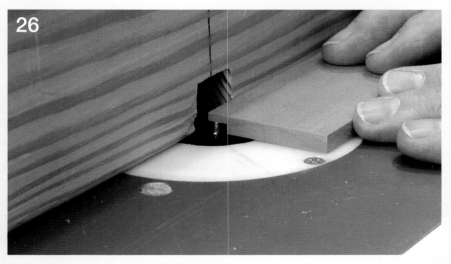

one of those ruined earlier lids) to push the workpiece through, which helps keep it square to the fence.

With the rabbet milled, rip the two sides to their 1¾" height. (Fig. 25) By milling the larger workpiece before cutting the final parts to size, not only is it easier, but you also don't have to worry about any tear-out from that rabbet since you've cut fresh, clean edges.

Mill a ¼" rabbet ⅛" deep on the bottom edge of each of the sides to accommodate the ¼" bottom insert, as in Fig. 26. This rabbet will match up with the ones you cut earlier in the bottom edges of the card box ends.

To make cards easier to draw from the box, create finger openings. For this box, I've cut two openings on each side of what will be the draw pile of cards, and a single opening on the opposite end piece of what will be the discard pile. However, if the card game you make this box for doesn't allow players to draw from the discard side, you can opt to skip an opening there. Or, if you want you can put openings around the card box on all four sides. How you arrange these openings is up to you.

27

Use the pattern provided on the previous page to locate the openings, and then make the curved portion with a 1¼" Forstner bit on the drill press. (Fig. 27) Now head to the band saw (or use a jigsaw or scroll saw) to make the vertical cuts as in Fig. 28. Finally, clean up and smooth the openings with a spindle sander. You'll note in Fig. 29 that I've made this easier by taping the two sides together and sanding both openings at the same time.

Now, assemble the card box with glue and clamps as in Fig. 30, but go easy on the clamping pressure! Those openings won't take a lot of stress (nor do they really even need a lot of pressure for a good joint). When the assembly is dry, apply glue to the bottom rabbets, drop the ¼" cherry bottom insert into place, and clamp up.

Finally, glue the divider in place and clamp things up again. (Figs. 31 & 32)

When the fully assembly card box has dried, give it a good sanding inside and out. I put a slight roundover on the outside top edge of each end piece that I think adds a nice profile, but you can leave those top edges square if you'd prefer.

Apply the finish of your choice, and add felt that matches what you put in the main box for a complementary effect.

28

29

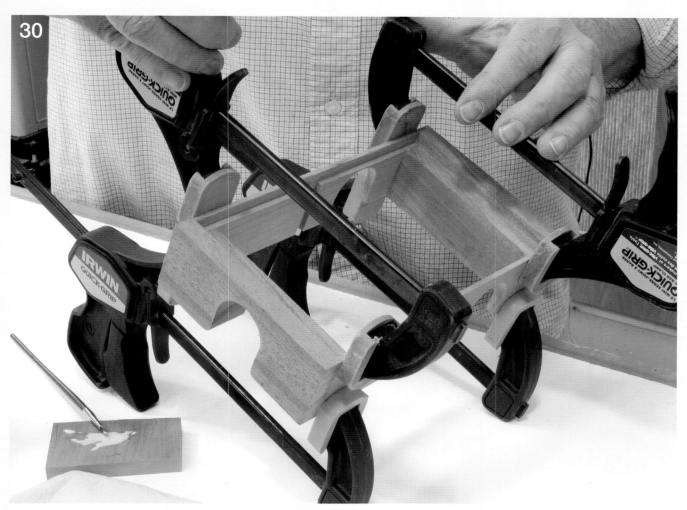

19 VERTICAL JEWELRY BOX

NO PUBLICATION CLAIMING TO BE A HAND-book of box building would be complete without a jewelry box. My first thought was to present a traditional jewelry box — low and rectangular, hinged lift-up lid, maybe an interior tray — but in all honesty that pretty much describes any hinged box. Indeed, I've already included a couple like that intended for other purposes, but easily used for jewelry. So, for this volume's entry I decided to go with something a bit different: a vertical jewelry box in the form of a small, adaptable cabinet with drawers.

I wanted contrasting wood species and so decided to use the same mix as in Kim's Christmas Box, walnut with spalted maple accents. This box uses a couple types of joinery, including doweled butt joints, traditional rabbets, grooves, panel book-matching, and a form of pseudo dado joints that'll be easier to show you than to explain.

This cabinet is a study in symmetry. Its slanted sides are obviously symmetrical left-to-right and the three drawers are the same width and height, but what might not be readily apparent is that I've repeated some measurements throughout. For example, the three drawers total 6" in height, which is exactly how wide the cabinet is at the base. The cabinet itself measures 4¾" front-to-back, which is exactly how wide the back panel insert is.

To contradict the symmetry a bit, I used a single piece of spalted maple cut into the individual false fronts on the drawers, with the grain flowing steadily through all three of them. I didn't want book-matching in this case — I wanted the random grain and spalting patterns to be the only overtly asymmetrical part of the box — but that rear insert panel I noted a moment ago is a piece of book-matched maple.

What did I mean by adaptable earlier? Well, you don't have to use it as a jewelry box, of course, but you can also alter the components in any way you like. Enlarge or increase the number of drawers; make the box taller, wider or deeper; instead of a single row of drawers, you could make two rows; or maybe a row of drawers on one side, and a hinged door on the other. You can do all of that and still keep the same basic form, style and proportions.

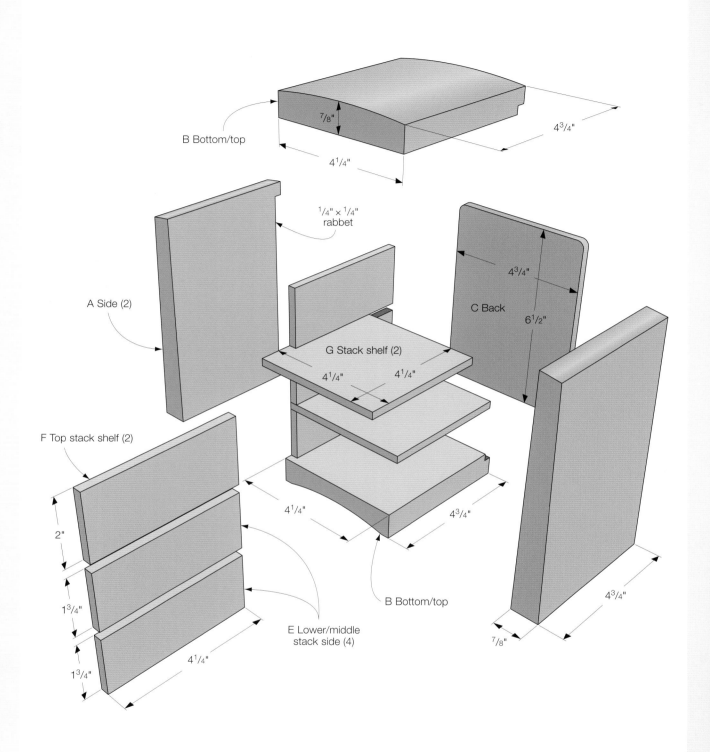

B Bottom/top

$^{7}/_{8}$"

$4^{1}/_{4}$"

$4^{3}/_{4}$"

$^{1}/_{4}$" × $^{1}/_{4}$"
rabbet

A Side (2)

C Back

$4^{3}/_{4}$"

$6^{1}/_{2}$"

G Stack shelf (2)

$4^{1}/_{4}$" $4^{1}/_{4}$"

F Top stack shelf (2)

2"

$1^{3}/_{4}$"

$1^{3}/_{4}$"

$4^{1}/_{4}$"

$4^{3}/_{4}$"

B Bottom/top

E Lower/middle
stack side (4)

$4^{1}/_{4}$"

$4^{3}/_{4}$"

$^{7}/_{8}$"

REFERENCE	QUANTITY	PART	STOCK	THICKNESS	(mm)	WIDTH	(mm)	LENGTH	(mm)	COMMENTS
Main Box										
A	2	sides	walnut	$7/8$	(22)	$4^3/4$	(121)	$7^3/4$	(197)	
B	2	top/bottom	walnut	$7/8$	(22)	$4^3/4$	(121)	$4^1/4$	(108)	
C	1	back	spalted maple	$1/4$	(6)	$4^3/4$	(121)	$6^1/2$	(165)	
D	8	dowels	hardwood	$1/4$	(6)	diameter		$3/4$	(19)	
E	4	lower/mid stack sides	walnut	$1/4$	(6)	$1^3/4$	(119)	$4^1/4$	(108)	
F	2	top stack sides	walnut	$1/4$	(6)	2	(51)	$4^1/4$	(108)	
G	2	stack shelves	walnut	$1/4$	(6)	$4^1/4$	(108)	$4^1/4$	(108)	
Drawers										
H	6	sides	walnut	$1/4$	(6)	$1^3/4$	(45)	4	(102)	
I	6	fronts/backs	walnut	$1/4$	(6)	$1^3/4$	(45)	$3^3/4$	(95)	
J	3	bottoms	ply	$1/8$	(3)	$3^1/2$	(89)	4	(102)	
K	3	false fronts	spalted maple	$1/4$	(6)	2	(51)	$4^1/4$	(108)	

Additonal Supplies: brass knobs, padded ring bar.

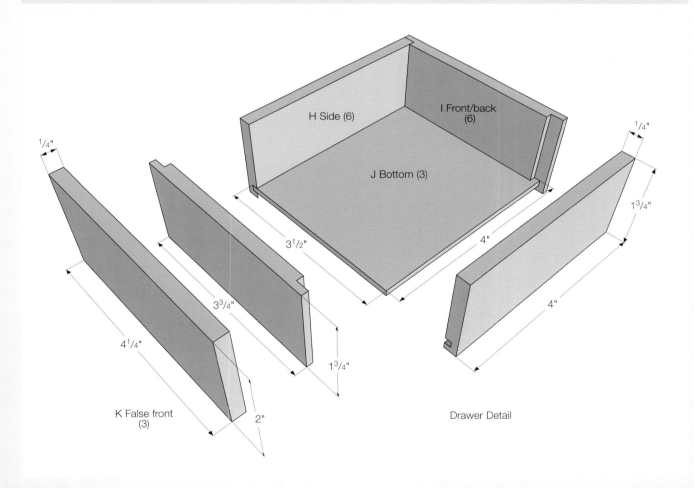

H Side (6)

I Front/back (6)

J Bottom (3)

$3^1/2$"

4"

$1/4$"

$1/4$"

$1^3/4$"

4"

$3^3/4$"

$1^3/4$"

$4^1/4$"

2"

K False front (3)

Drawer Detail

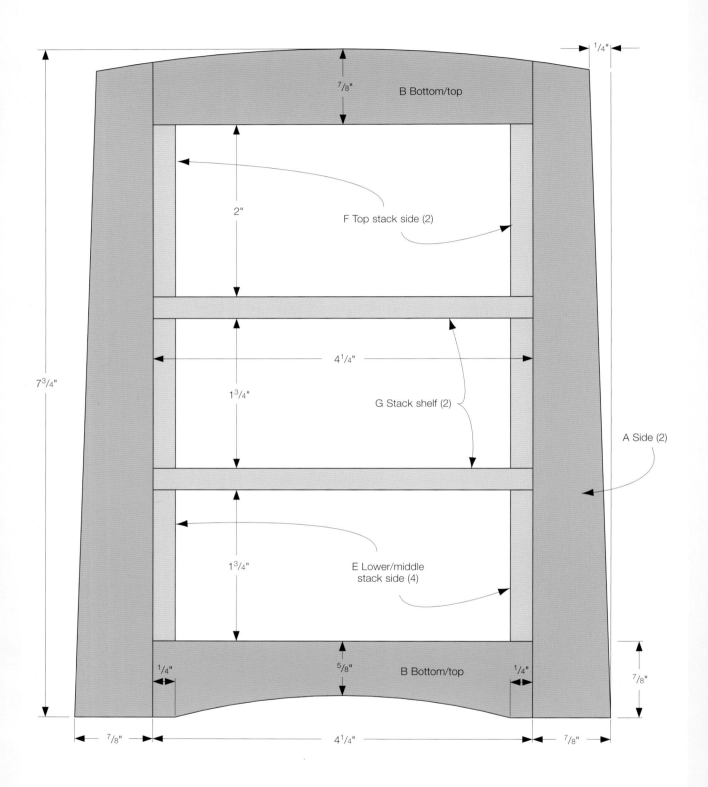

Construction

I started with 4/4 walnut that, once surfaced, came out to the ⁷⁄₈" stock I used for the cabinet. Although the cabinet is small, I wanted it to have some heft — I dislike having to hold a box steady in order to remove a drawer, but this box is heavy enough that it won't skitter around when pulling out a drawer. The project also requires a good bit of ¼" walnut for the drawers and other components, so your first step is to mill some stock down to ¼" (Fig. 1) With the stock milled, begin cutting your components for the main box cabinet by cutting the two sides as well as the top and bottom. (Fig. 2)

This cabinet is assembled with butt joints, which, as I've noted a couple of times already, are perfectly acceptable joints for box making. But because this is a heavy box I've

decided to reinforce the joinery a bit with ¼" dowels. However, because we'll taper the cabinet sides and curve the top in a later step, you have to be careful with the dowel placement — you don't want to cut into those dowels later when shaping the cabinet.

Draw a line ¼" from the bottom edge on both sides of the box top, with another pair of lines ¼" from the top of the box bottom. By placing the dowels on these lines it'll put them outside the area we'll be cutting later. Use packing tape to join the top and bottom, and you'll find that the combined thicknesses allow the two pieces to rest perfectly vertical on your drill press table for exact 90-degree holes. Drill two ¼" holes ½" deep on your lines on each side of both pieces, placing the holes about 1" from the ends of the pieces as in Fig. 3.

The key to accurate dowel joinery is to correctly place the matching holes in the adjoining components; get these holes wrong and the pieces won't line up. This is a simple task with little accessories called dowel centers. With the holes drilled in one component, slip the dowel centers into the holes (these centers come in most common dowel sizes). Put the two components against a square edge, such as a table saw fence, and press the two pieces together, as in Fig. 4. Take a close look at Fig. 5, and you can see how the dowel center creates small dimples in the adjoining box sides, showing you exactly where to drill. These things are great; if you don't have a set, get one. With the locations marked, drill these matching holes ¼" deep.

When the assembly has dried, put a bit of glue into the holes and insert the dowels, as in Fig. 6. Then, apply glue to the edges of the pieces and assemble the box cabinet, clamping it up until dry. (Fig. 7)

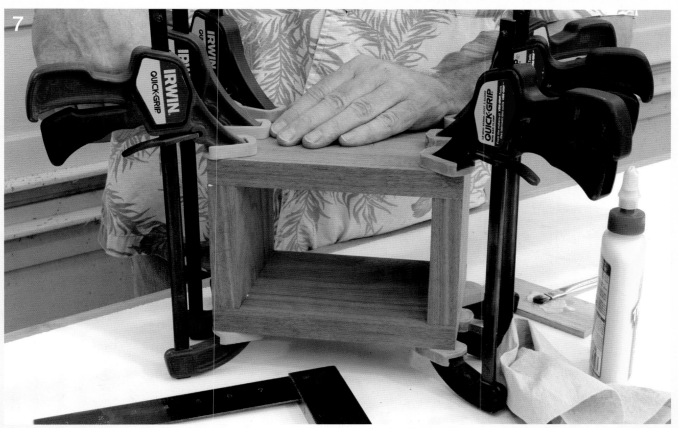

This box has a rear insert. In earlier projects with this type of rear panel we created the rabbets before assembling the box. However, those boxes didn't feature butt joinery, which makes creating rabbets difficult before assembly. Instead, when the assembly is dry use your router table to rout a continuous ¼" × ¼" rabbet around the inside edges of the box back as in Fig. 8.

Cutting a rabbet in this manner results in curved corners — routers can't cut square corners — so you can do one of two things. Sometimes, I prefer to use a chisel to square the rabbet corners in the box and insert a back panel with corners that are likewise square. But for this box I wanted the curved corners, so instead I cut out the panel to the dimensions on the Cut List, and rounded those corners for a perfect fit as you can see in Fig. 9.

Creating the "Stack"

One of the most common ways to create a cabinet with multiple drawers is to mill dados on the inside that will accept shelf-like dividers; the drawers then slide in easily on these shelves. We did that for the Spool Cabinet box earlier, and in fact you'll see this type of joinery in larger furniture such as chests and dressers. However, those dados are visible in the finished piece and I didn't want that for this box; I wanted just the smooth flow of those three spalted maple drawer fronts.

But to keep them hidden would require milling a very accurate series of stopped dados on the interior of the box, which would be time-consuming and difficult. Alternatively, you could construct an inner box with through dados that would slip inside the main box. Again, this would take a while. Several years ago I came up with a method that is fast and easy, and looks exactly like milled dados. The idea came to me when I wanted a built-in bookcase fitted to a tall, narrow alcove in our bedroom. The alcove was taller than the stock I had on hand, so instead of having continuous sides, I cut a series of shorter pieces the same length as the spaces between the shelves.

How this works is that two side pieces go up first at the bottom, which are topped by a shelf. Follow that with two more side pieces, another shelf and so on till you have a "shelf stack" of the necessary height. There's no joinery at all involved, but the juxtaposition of a side piece, shelf edge and the next side piece simulates a dado joint; it's very strong, secure and looks just like a dado. I've used this trick for years and can honestly say I came up with it on my own — at least, I'd never seen or heard of it before — so maybe someday they'll name it after me. Or not.

In any event, we'll do a shelf stack for this box that'll be indistinguishable from perfect dados. Begin by cutting your stacking side pieces to size per the Cut List. Be sure to cut them so that the grain goes across the short dimension; when stacked, you want the grain to be vertical like the rest of the box. Insert a pair of stack sides into the box and face-glue them in place as in Fig. 10. When the glueup is dry, top the two pieces with a shelf to which you've applied

10

a bit of glue on the bottom edges, as in Fig. 11. Now add two more stack sides, another shelf, and the final two stack sides. As you can see in Fig. 12, the finished shelf stack is almost indistinguishable from dados.

You'll notice that the top two stack sides are ¼" taller than the lower ones. This is because there's no top shelf for another drawer, so these top stack sides are taller to compensate. Since all three drawer fronts are 2" high, the three drawer openings have to be the same; higher stack sides at the top allow this.

Make the Drawers

Now, make the drawers to fit the jewelry box cabinet. The rabbeted drawer fronts/backs (Part I) aren't large, so as we did with the Game Box project, let's cut and mill these all at once from a larger workpiece, then cut out the individual parts. Measuring with the grain, cut workpieces 3¾"-wide and long enough to make several components. (Fig. 13) My walnut was wide enough that I could get three components out of each, so I needed two.

With a dado set in your table saw, or a straight bit in the router table, mill ¼"-wide rabbets ⅛" deep on each side of the workpieces, as in Fig.

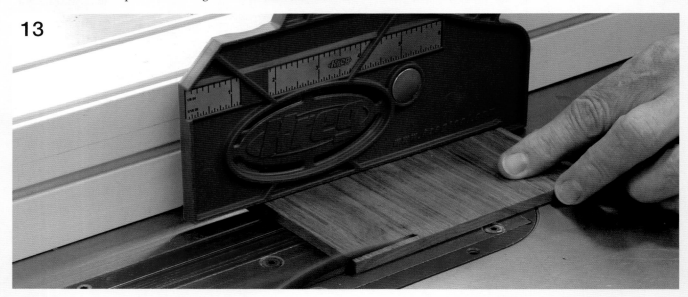

14. Then rip the drawer front/backs to their final height of 1¾". (Fig. 15)

Cut the drawer side workpieces to 1¾"-wide, but don't cut them to length until after cutting a continuous ⅛" groove ⅛" from one edge of the stock as in Fig. 16. With the saw still set up, cut the same groove in the bottoms of the six drawer front/backs. These slots will accept the ⅛" plywood drawer bottoms.

Cut the drawer bottoms to size per the Cut List and cut the drawer sides to length, then do a dry assembly of each box as in Fig. 17, checking to be sure the plywood bottom is sized correctly and fits as it should. When you're satisfied with the fit, assemble with glue and clamp up. These drawer boxes are small, and so you don't need a lot of clamping pressure. Small clamps are best, but some stiff rubber bands will also do the trick.

While the drawer assemblies are drying, cut the box cabinet's curved top, curved bottom detail and tapered sides to shape on the band saw. (Fig. 18) Give the cabinet a good sanding — a disc sander easily handles the curved top, a spindle sander works

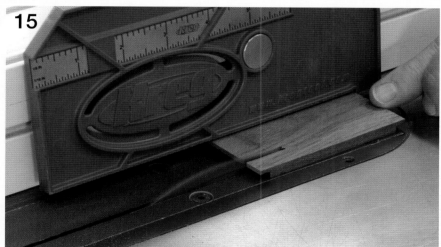

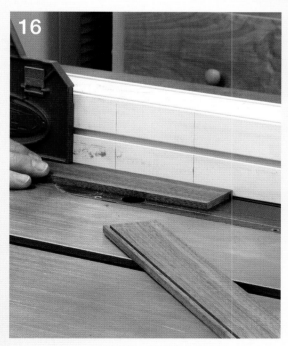

best for the inside curve of the bottom detail, and a disc sander makes short work of the curved top. Finish-sand the entire cabinet with a random orbit sander or by hand, working up through increasingly finer grits to achieve a smooth surface.

Test all three of the drawers as in Fig. 19, and adjust their fit as necessary by sanding. Note in this photo that I've temporarily added some masking tape "pulls" to make it easier to get the drawers out should the fit be too tight.

Cut out the three false fronts to size per the Cut List, making sure that if you're using spalted or other figured wood that the direction of the figuring runs vertically for best appearance. These fronts overhang the drawer by ¼" at the top and on both sides to cover the internal shelf stack, so you'll need to mark them carefully so the drawers are perfectly centered when face-glued together. Do this by butting the three drawer fronts face-down against a square edge — again, I'm using the fence on my table saw — and mark the backs at ¼" from each edge as in Fig. 20.

Apply glue to the front of each drawer and place it on the back side of the drawer front so that they're flush with the bottom edge and centered exactly between your marks, then clamp the fronts in place till dry. (Fig. 21) Spring clamps or ratchet clamps work best for this. Be careful as you apply pressure that the front doesn't slide — your figuring will be misaligned if it does (and the drawer won't fit flush into the opening on the front of the box), and you won't be able to fix it.

When the drawers are dry, give them a good final sanding. Drill holes appropriate for the pull or knob of your choice in the exact center of each drawer front. The last step is to set up the drawer interiors however you like. If you plan to use this box for any purpose other than a jewelry box, you can probably just leave the box interiors open or perhaps add a liner on the bottom. For use a jewelry box, consider adding dividers or other means of organizing jewelry. My wife likes rings, so I've designated two

18

19

20

of the drawers to accommodate padded ring bars. These are velvet-covered foam bars formed with slots in the top into which rings can be slid in and held securely.

If you plan to include commercially available ring bars, be sure to order yours before you decide on the dimensions of your box. The ring bar I got measures 3¼" wide and I've sized my drawers accordingly for a perfect fit. These bars are easy to cut; as you can see in Fig. 22, a sharp serrated knife does the trick. The knife I'm using in this photo is a bread knife, and cuts the bar with a nice clean edge.

Once you've sized any inserts, set them aside and apply the finish of your choice. This box has a Danish oil finish, but if you want a higher gloss consider polyurethane, any wiping varnish or shellac. With the finish dry and rubbed out the way you like it, install the knobs or pulls.

One last note on the drawers. Each of the false fronts is exactly 2" high for a vertically symmetrical appearance, but you've undoubtedly noticed that the drawer openings aren't the same size. Because the two lower drawers have a shelf above them for the next drawer, their openings are 1¾" high. The uppermost drawer opening, however, has no shelf above it, so that opening is 2". I've made all three drawer boxes the same height at 1¾", but if you prefer you can make that top drawer a full 2" to take advantage of the larger opening. You'll have a bit more depth capacity for that drawer, but the appearance from the front of the box will remain the same.

163

EVERY PARENT KNOWS THAT CHILDREN LOVE boxes. That's because every parent has purchased at least one expensive gift in a child's life, only to watch the child delightfully play with the empty box the expensive item came in. This project caters to kids' love of boxes, and incorporates some shape-recognition activities as well with the accompanying colorful blocks.

Chances are good that toddlers will put this box through the wringer, so we'll make it plenty durable with ½" stock and box joints. As promised earlier in the Pencil Box project, we'll use the table saw this time to cut the box joints with an easy-to-make jig.

20 CHILD'S BOX

Construction

Begin by installing a ½" dado set into your table saw. Use your ½" stock to set the height, as in Fig. 1. As I did with the Pencil Box project, I've set that blade just a hair over ½" so the fingers will err on the long side — those can easily be sanded flush for a perfectly smooth joint.

Now, create a sacrificial fence for your miter gauge by cutting a ½" × ½" slot in the bottom edge, as in Fig. 2. Locate this slot so there's enough room on both sides for the stock you'll be milling. In this case, I've allowed about 7", which will fully support the 6½"-wide workpieces for this box.

Glue a short length of ½"-wide stock into the slot you've just created, which will act as an index pin to register your cuts. In Fig. 3, you can see that I've made this pin a bit shorter than ½". This will allow the workpiece to seat properly even if sawdust accumulates on top of the pin.

Offset the pin in your fence by exactly ½" from the blade, as in Fig. 4. I've used a bit more of the same ½" stock I used for the pin to set the distance to ensure that it will be precise. With the fence set exactly, attach it solidly to your miter gauge. Your miter gauge probably has holes that allow a sacrificial fence to be attached from the back with screws.

From this point, the process of cutting the joints is the same as for the Pencil Box, with the first cut starting with an "A" side piece against the fence. Butt the top edge against

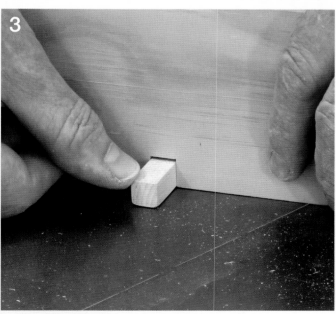

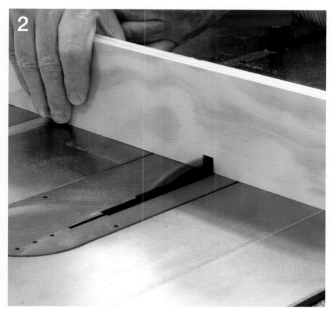

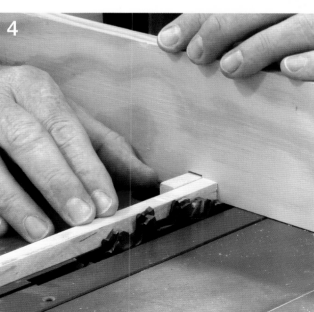

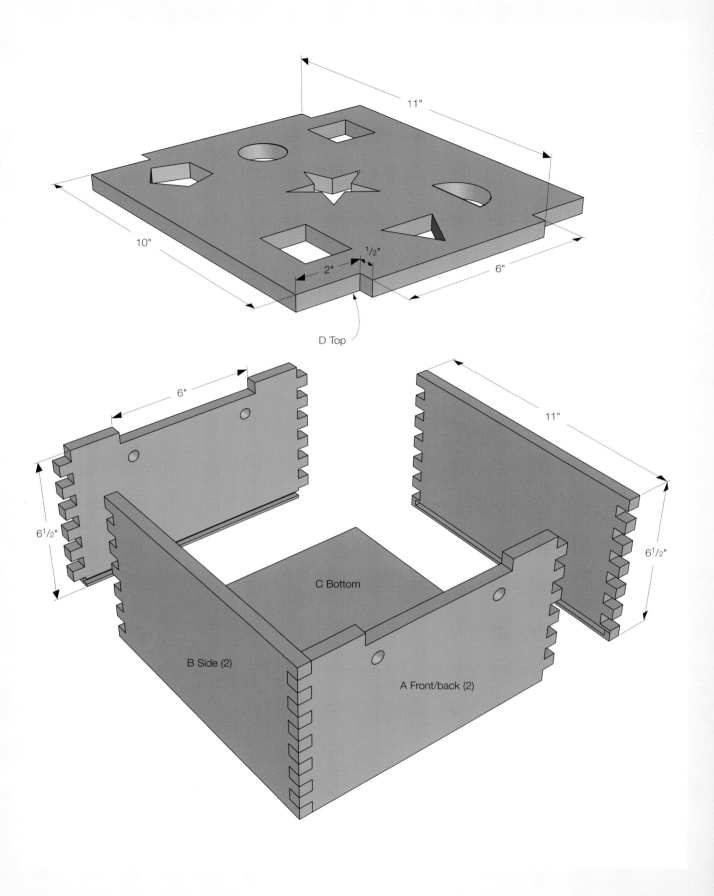

11"

10"

2"

1/2"

6"

D Top

6"

6 1/2"

11"

6 1/2"

C Bottom

B Side (2)

A Front/back (2)

REFERENCE	QUANTITY	PART	STOCK	THICKNESS	(mm)	WIDTH	(mm)	LENGTH	(mm)	COMMENTS
A	2	front/back	poplar	1/2	(13)	6 1/2	(165)	11	(279)	
B	2	sides	poplar	1/2	(13)	6 1/2	(165)	11	(279)	
C	1	bottom	plywood	1/4	(6)	10 1/2	(267)	10 1/2	(267)	
D	1	top	plywood	1/2	(13)	10	(254)	11	(279)	
E	2	handles	rope	3/8	(10)	diameter				

the index pin, and slide the fence and workpiece through the dado blade as in Fig. 5.

Lift the workpiece off the jig and pull the fence smoothly back till it clears the dado blade. Reposition the workpiece, moving it one notch over so the first cut rests atop the index pin, and slide everything through the blade again as in Fig. 6. As with the Pencil Box, repeat each cut-move-cut maneuver until you've finished all the fingers on that end of the workpiece. Now, flip the workpiece over end-for-end, once again with the top edge against the index pin, and cut the joints on the opposite end.

Flip the workpiece over side-for-side, orienting the opposite face against the fence. This should put the top edge toward the center on the other side of the index pin. Place the top finger over the index pin (Fig. 7) to create a spacer. Place a "B" side piece against the fence with the top edge butted against the spacer created by the top edge of the "A" piece.

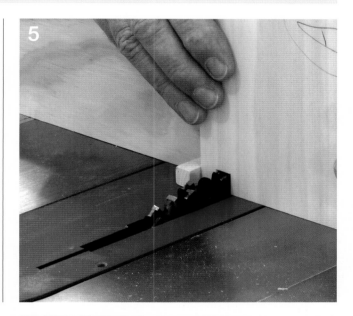

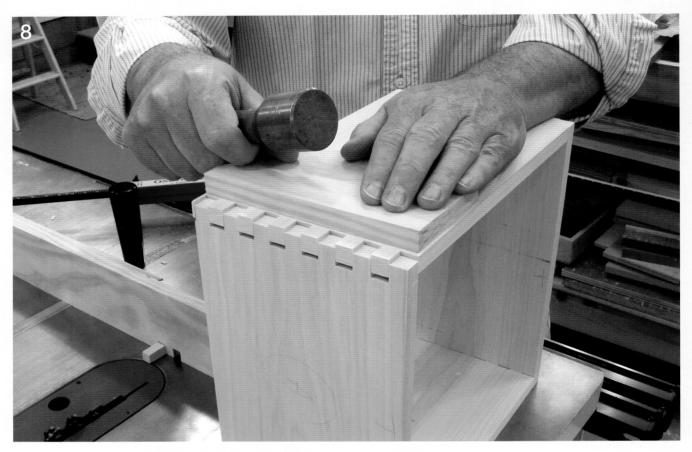

Hold everything securely — clamp the workpieces to the fence if necessary — and slide everything through the dado blade to make the first cut on the top edge of the "B" piece.

Take both workpieces off the jig and set the "A" piece aside. Pull the fence back, move the "B" workpiece over so the first cut is against the index pin, and proceed down the end of the piece to complete all the fingers as before. Repeat the process for each remaining workpiece.

When cutting joints, I'm a big proponent of doing a dry-fit to check everything out before going any further on a project. (Fig. 8) For this box there are a lot of fingers and lot of wood sliding on wood, so the fit may be a bit tight. If so, tap the joint into place, using a piece of scrap to protect the surface. If the fit is really tight, a light sanding of the fingers should ease things up. Sand sparingly, however: You just want to make the parts go together easier, you don't want a loose joint.

This box requires ¼" grooves cut ¼" deep on the inside faces to accommodate the plywood bottom, and we'll do that on the router table as we did for the Pencil Box. Because they have a space nearest the bottom edges, the "B" pieces are the easiest to do because you can just slide the workpieces straight through to cut the groove, as in Fig. 9. The groove openings are hidden inside the joint, and so unseen from the outside of the box. For that reason, you could also cut the grooves in your "B" pieces on the table saw with a ¼" dado set, or multiple passes with a standard blade.

For the "A" pieces, however, you have a joint finger nearest the bottom edges, so you need to make a stopped groove that ends before cutting all the way through. Can't do that on the table saw, hence my preference for the router table for doing all the grooves. You'll want this groove to end about ⅛" before coming out the tip of the finger, so make start and stop marks on your fence to use as a guide for keeping the groove inside the workpiece.

Turn on the router, and then hold the workpiece over the bit in line with your start mark as in Fig. 10. Carefully lower the workpiece onto the bit. Now, slide the workpiece along the fence to cut the groove until you reach your "stop" mark, then lift the workpiece off the bit. (Fig. 11) If lifting a workpiece off a spinning bit makes you nervous, hold the workpiece in place, turn off the router, and wait till the bit spins down to lift the workpiece.

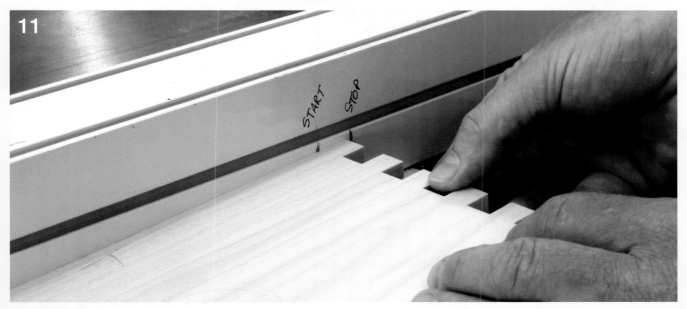

Repeat the procedure to cut the groove in the remaining "A" workpiece. In Fig. 12, you can see how these two grooves "meet" inside the joint when the box is assembled. Because you cut the stopped groove ⅛" from the end of the finger, the rounded portion clears the end of the other groove.

Drill a pair of holes on each side for the rope handles, sized to accommodate the rope you plan to use. I like to combine procedures with identical parts whenever possible — it saves time and ensures that whatever you're doing is exactly the same in both pieces — so you can see in Fig. 13 that I've taped the two sides together before drilling.

Now, mark out the ½" × 6" lid mortises, centering them on the top edges of the taped-up sides. I'm doing this on the band saw as in Fig. 14, but you can also do this with a jigsaw or scroll saw. Alternatively, you can cut this by orienting the sides vertically, and making a series of overlapping cuts on the router table or with a dado set in your table saw. After cutting the mortises, sand them smooth. In Fig. 15, a bit of sandpaper wrapped

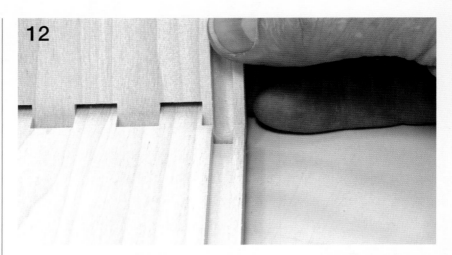

around a thin hardwood scrap handles the task quickly.

Finally, cut the 10½" × 10½" plywood bottom to size, and give all the completed components a good sanding. Apply glue to all the joint fingers, then slip the bottom into one of the grooves and assemble the box around it. For larger boxes, I prefer band clamps to pull everything securely together until the glue cures. In Fig. 16, I'm using a set of box-joint cauls. These plastic cauls have ½" pads that provide even pressure on each of the fingers, making for a tight, space-free joint.

When everything has dried, remove the clamps and give the exterior of the box a good sanding, paying special attention that the fingers at each corner are flush and smooth.

Prepare the box lid by cutting a piece of ½" plywood to size. Solid wood isn't a good choice here — a single, loose piece of solid wood may warp over time — but plywood is very strong and remains stable. Be sure to go with a higher-quality material, such as Baltic birch plywood, that is void-free. Give the lid a good

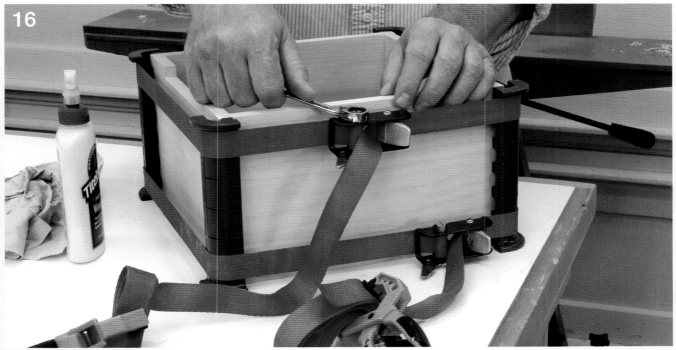

sanding on both faces and all edges, and set it aside for now.

This is the point in the project where you can really let your imagination take over. As you can see in the lead photo, I've designed the activity feature of this box with wood blocks cut into various geometric shapes, each of which fits through matching cutouts in the lid. However, you could just as easily make your blocks shaped like animals, birds, dinosaurs — anything you want. You could also cruise through a large toy store and find stacking plastic blocks in a host of shapes, and use those if you prefer. I had used a large slab of 2"-thick poplar for a recent project and had a decent chunk left over, and opted to cut my own blocks from that. I drew geometric shapes in pairs on this workpiece — triangles, squares, pentagons, etc. — and cut them out on the band saw. (Fig. 17) I ended up making seven pairs of different shapes, 14 blocks in all.

Whether you make your own blocks or buy them from a toy store, lay one of each shape atop your lid and trace around them, as in Fig. 18. To make the

opening a bit easier for toddlers, make your tracings a bit oversized so that once the openings are cut out the blocks will slip effortlessly through.

I've recommended a scroll saw a couple of times in earlier projects as a possible tool for cutting detailed shapes, but up till now have always opted for something else. And although you could use a jig saw or coping saw here, for these cutouts a scroll saw is really the tool of choice, which is why I went out and bought one before starting this project (Fig. 19). Scroll saw blades easily make all the sharp turns and tight curves you'll need to make these cutouts, and they do it with a very fine cut requiring minimal sanding.

Notch the 10" sides of the lid to create tenons centered on each side. You can see in Fig. 20 how the lid then drops into the mortises, and is recessed smoothly into the opening of the box.

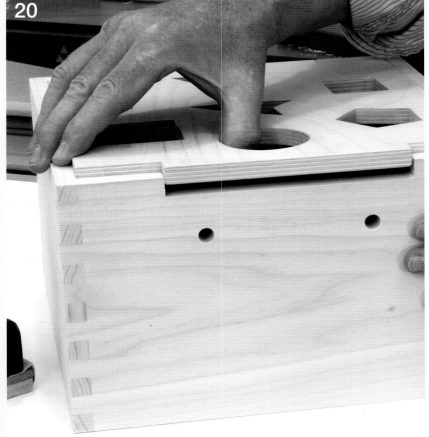

Give the box and lid several coats of clear finish. Because this box will likely take a lot of abuse, I've opted for polyurethane for good protection. For the blocks, feel free to indulge yourself and paint them up with whatever bright colors you like. Since these blocks will likely find their way into little mouths as often as they will the cutouts in the box, be sure to use a nontoxic paint.

The next-to-last step is to make this box easy to carry around with a pair of colorful rope handles. I've used ³⁄₈" rope made of soft nylon, and recommend you do the same — if the rope frays (it will, eventually) — the fraying will be very soft and won't hurt small hands. Avoid rope that is extremely stiff, as frayed threads can be rough; use only a soft, very flexible rope. Cut a length for each side and slip the ends into the holes, then tie tight knots on the inside of the box to keep the handles in place.

The last step is the most enjoyable of all. Give the box to a small child and start having fun. I guarantee they won't play with the box it came in.

SUPPLIERS

ADAMS & KENNEDY —
THE WOOD SOURCE
6178 Mitch Owen Rd.
P.O. Box 700
Manotick, ON
Canada K4M 1A6
613-822-6800
www.wood-source.com
Wood supply

BUSY BEE TOOLS
130 Great Gulf Dr.
Concord, ON
Canada L4K 5W1
1-800-461-2879
www.busybeetools.com
Woodworking tools and supplies

CONSTANTINE'S WOOD
CENTER OF FLORIDA
1040 E. Oakland Park Blvd.
Fort Lauderdale, FL 33334
800-443-9667
www.constantines.com
Tools, woods, veneers, hardware

DOVER DESIGNS, LLC
P.O. Box 3644
Hagerstown, MD 21742
301-733-0909
www.www.doverdesignsllc.com
Suppliers of fine inlay, borders, wood lines and marquetry designs

FENTON ART GLASS
700 Elizabeth Street
Williamstown, WV 26187
304-375-6122
http://www.fentonartglass.com
Glass Beads as shown in the Bead Box

FRANK PAXTON
LUMBER COMPANY
5701 W. 66th St.
Chicago, IL 60638
800-323-2203
www.paxtonwood.com
Wood, hardware, tools, books

HIGHLAND WOODWORKING
1045 North Highland Ave. NE
Atlanta, GA 30306
www.highlandwoodworking.
com
Tools, woodworking supplies, books

HORTON BRASSES INC.
49 Nooks Hill Road
Cromwell, CT 06416
800-754-9127
www.horton-brasses.com
Fine reproduction brass and iron hardware

KLINGSPOR ABRASIVES INC.
2555 Tate Blvd. SE
Hickory, N.C. 28602
800-645-5555
www.klingspor.com
Sandpaper of all kinds

LEE VALLEY TOOLS LTD.
P.O. Box 1780
Ogdensburg, NY 13669-6780
800-871-8158 (U.S.)
800-267-8767 (Canada)
www.leevalley.com
Woodworking tools and hardware

LONDONDERRY BRASSES LTD.
P.O. Box 415
Cochranville, PA 19330
610-593-6239
londonderry-brasses.com
Furniture hardware

LOWE'S COMPANIES, INC.
P.O. Box 1111
North Wilkesboro, NC 28656
800-445-6937
www.lowes.com
Woodworking tools, supplies and hardware

PEN MAKING SUPPLIES
P.O. Box 607
Peapack, NJ 07977
(908) 204-0095
www.penmakingsupplies.com
Grecian combination doors, coin slots

R.P & COMPANY HISTORICAL
COIN BANKS
P.O. Box 269
Errol, NH 03579
(603) 482-3252
www.rpcompany.com
Two-dial and Grecian combination doors, number decals, slots

ROCKLER WOODWORKING
AND HARDWARE
4365 Willow Dr.
Medina, MN 55340
800-279-4441
www.rockler.com
Grecian keyed doors, coin slots for P.O. Box & ring keep for Jewelry box

TOOL TREND LTD.
140 Snow Blvd. Unit 1
Concord, ON
Canada L4K 4C1
416-663-8665
Woodworking tools and hardware

JOHN WILSON & ERIC PINTAR,
LLC
406 E. Broadway
Charlotte, MI 48813
(517)543-5325
www.shakerovalbox.com
Materials for making Shaker boxes, including forms and patterns, hardwood bands, lid/bottom inserts, tacks and soaking trays.

WOODCRAFT SUPPLY LLC
1177 Rosemar Rd.
P.O. Box 1686
Parkersburg, WV 26102
800-535-4482
www.woodcraft.com
Woodworking hardware

WOODWORKER'S HARDWARE
P.O. Box 180
Sauk Rapids, MN 56379-0180
800-383-0130
www.wwhardware.com
Woodworking hardware

WOODWORKER'S SUPPLY
1108 N. Glenn Rd.
Casper, WY 82601
800-645-9292
http://woodworker.com
Woodworking tools and accessories, finishing supplies, books and plans

Also from author A.J. Hamler, and *Popular Woodworking Books*

Must-Know Info to Attract and Keep the Birds You Want

Birdhouse projects are very satisfying, making them popular with both avid and amateur woodworkers. They can be assembled quickly and with inexpensive materials. And while they are not high furniture, the finished project is on constant display for all to see. This book features birdhouses designed to not only look natural — with careful wood selection and an unobtrusive appearance — but fits the house to the bird itself, addressing the needs of individual species. The feeding requirements of various types of birds are also discussed, with an examination of the best ways to present food to them. And for those who want more challenging projects, several colorful and whimsical birdhouse designs are presented.

Available at shopwoodworking.com

Ideas. Instruction. Inspiration.

These and other great **Popular Woodworking** products are available at your local bookstore, woodworking store or online supplier.

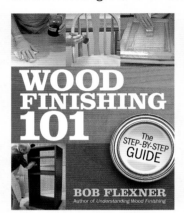

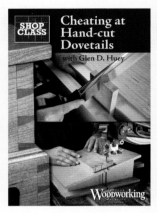

WOOD FINISHING 101
By Bob Flexner

Wood finishing doesn't have to be complicated or confusing. Wood Finishing 101 boils it down to simple step-by-step instructions and pictures on how to finish common woods using widely-available finishing materials. Bob Flexner has been writing about and teaching wood finishing for over 20 years.

paperback • 128 pages

WEEKEND WOODWORKER'S PROJECT COLLECTION

This book has 40 projects from which to choose and, depending on the level of your woodworking skills, any of them can be completed in one or two weekends. Projects include: a game box, jewelry box, several styles of bookcases and shelves, mirrors, picture frames and more.

paperback • 256 pages

POPULAR WOODWORKING MAGAZINE

Whether learning a new hobby or perfecting your craft, *Popular Woodworking Magazine* has expert information to teach the skill, not just the project. Find the latest issue on newsstands, or you can order online at popularwoodworking.com.

SHOPCLASS VIDEOS

From drafting, to dovetails and even how to carve a ball-and-claw foot, our Shop Class Videos let you see the lesson as if you were standing right there.

Available at shopwoodworking.com
DVD & Instant download

POPULAR WOODWORKING'S VIP PROGRAM

Get the Most Out of Woodworking!

Join the Woodworker's Bookshop VIP program today for the tools you need to advance your woodworking abilities. Your one-year paid renewal membership includes:

- *Popular Woodworking Magazine* (1 year/7 issue U.S. subscription - A $21.97 Value)
- *Popular Woodworking Magazine CD* — Get all issues of *Popular Woodworking Magazine* from 2006 to today on one CD (A $64.95 Value!)
- The Best of Shops & Workbenches CD — 62 articles on workbenches, shop furniture, shop organization and the essential jigs and fixtures published in *Popular Woodworking* and *Woodworking Magazine* ($15.00 Value!)

- 20% Members-Only Savings on 6-Month Subscription for Shop Class OnDemand
- 10% Members-Only Savings at Shopwoodworking.com
- 10% Members-Only Savings on FULL PRICE Registration for Woodworking In America Conference (Does Not Work with Early Bird Price)
- and more....

Visit **popularwoodworking.com** to see more woodworking information by the experts, learn about our digital subscription and sign up to receive our weekly newsletter at popularwoodworking.com/newsletters/

  FOLLOW POPULAR WOODWORKING